ENGLISH SONNETS

ENGLISH SONNETS

EDITED, WITH INTRODUCTION
AND NOTES
BY
A. T. QUILLER-COUCH

Granger Index Reprint Series

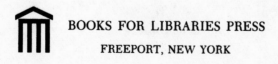
BOOKS FOR LIBRARIES PRESS
FREEPORT, NEW YORK

R69-01905

First Published 1897
Reprinted 1968

LIBRARY OF CONGRESS CATALOG CARD NUMBER:

68-58821

MANUFACTURED BY HALLMARK LITHOGRAPHERS, INC. IN THE U.S.A.

INTRODUCTION

" *The Sonnet—both thing and name—comes
to us from the Italian.*" [1] *Etymologically,*
sonnetto (*from* sonare, "*to play upon an
instrument*") *is a little poem with instru-
mental accompaniment : just as* canzone *is a
poem intended to be sung merely, and* ballata *a
poem accompanied with dancing.*

But as a matter of fact the earliest sonnetti
*discoverable have a proper precision of form to
which the ballad and song have never yet at-
tained, and, most likely, never will attain. We
cannot trace them back beyond the thirteenth
century : but the sonnets of Lodovico della
Vernaccia, Pier delle Vigne, Guido Guinicelli,*

[1] Mark Pattison. Introduction to the Sonnets of
John Milton.

v

INTRODUCTION

Jacopo da Lentino, Guittone d' Arezzo and others,[1] *mostly dating between* 1200 *and* 1250, *scarcely differ in structure from the sonnet which Petrarch practised and handed down as a model to the present day.* *We will discuss the structure by and by.*

Among these early Italians, Fra Guittone d' Arezzo—he was not a monk, but wore the prefix as a member of the half-religious, half-military order of Cavalieri di Santa Maria— *seems somehow to have walked off with the credit of having perfected the sonnet as an instrument: insomuch that Mr. Capel Lofft, who edited an anthology of sonnets early in the present century,*[2] *salutes him as the Columbus of poetic literature.* *With what justice we are asked to prefer him above his brethren does not quite appear.* *But it seems certain that he enjoyed a great reputation in his own day, and by it gave a certain* cachet *to the sonnet-form which he approved and employed.* *Dante himself* (1265 —1321), *who considered Fra Guittone an over-estimated person, uses the word " sonnet" of*

[1] The English reader will find some account of these early Italian singers, with illustrative translations of their work, in D. G. Rossetti's *Dante and his Circle*. Part II. Poets chiefly before Dante.

[2] Capel Lofft, *Laura* 1813-14.

INTRODUCTION

two forms of composition only ; and one of these, and by far the more usual, is Guittone's form ; the other being an arrangement of two sestets followed by two quatrains—with which we need not trouble ourselves. Guittone's form was finally lifted and sealed supreme by Petrarch's adoption (1304—1374), and as the Petrarcan we may henceforth speak of it.

The Petrarcan sonnet, then, has a matter and form of its own. In substance it is a reflective poem on love, or at least in some mood of love. It has a unity of its own, and must be the expression of a single thought or feeling. In structure it obeys the following rules :

1. It consists of fourteen lines ; each line having five beats or musical stresses.

2. The lines must rhyme : and in the disposition of its rhymes the sonnet divides into two systems, the first eight lines forming the major system, and the remaining six the minor.

The major system of eight lines, or two quatrains, is called the octave : the minor system of six lines, or two tercets, is called the sestet.

3. The octave must contain two rhyme-sounds only : and although in some Petrarcan sonnets

vii

we find these arranged in simple alternation (A B, A B, A B, A B), *in an octave of the normal type lines* 1, 4, 5, 8 *will rhyme together, and lines* 2, 3, 6, 7 *will rhyme together upon a different note* (A B B A, A B B A).

4. *The sestet may contain either two or three rhyme-sounds : but none of these must repeat or resemble the rhyme-sounds of the octave. And some hold that, to be perfectly normal, the sestet should have the division between its tercets clearly marked : thus* e. g. *we may have* C D C, D C D, *or* C D E, C D E, *besides other variations.*

5. *In expressing what the poet has to say, the sonnet must adapt itself to the intention of its length or structure. The octave should present the poet's idea, the sestet apply it : or the octave should introduce and develop an image, the sestet give back the general reflection suggested by it. In either case there will be a marked pause between the two.*

Besides this indispensable pause, there should be—we may take it as a counsel of perfection and a rule subject to many conditions of expediency—two lesser pauses ; the first between the two quatrains of the octave, the second between the two tercets of the sestet. Thus a Petrarcan sonnet ordered upon a Platonic idea of perfection—upon a model " laid up somewhere in the heavens "—would run somewhat as follows : The first quatrain introduces *the poet's thought or mood: after a slight pause, " as of one who is turning over what has been said in the mind to enforce it further," the second quatrain* develops *it : then after a deep pause, the minor system opens, and the first tercet takes up the thought and* applies *it or* reveals a deeper suggestiveness ; *and the concluding tercet* sums up *the whole matter in a general reflection.*

Such then was the Petrarcan sonnet in matter and form ; and such in matter and form (subject to minor experiments and variations) the sonnet remained in the hands of Michael Angelo, Tasso, and the great Italians ; of Camoens ; and of Ronsard, Du Bellay and the early French sonneteers.

The first English sonnets appeared in the year 1557, *in the book commonly known as* Tottel's Miscellany. *It had for its formal title ' Songes and sonnettes written by the ryght honorable lorde Henry Howard, late earle of Surrey and other' : and was in fact the first and posthumous edition of the poems of the Earl of Surrey and Sir Thomas Wyat, with*

ix

*other pieces by contemporaries named and un-
named. The editor, Nicholas Grimald (whose
name suggests Grimaldi and an Italian
parentage [1]) avows the source of his poets' inspiration, and hopes by their experiments to
prove that "the English tongue can earn like
praise with the Italian and other."* Tottel's
Miscellany *marks the opening of an epoch in
the history of English song — an epoch of
Italian influence which lasted for more than
a century, and was not fairly superseded by
the influence of France until the Restoration.
Wyat and Surrey together brought the sonnet
into England : nor can we say positively of this
pair that one gave a lead to the other. But if
one must have the credit, the probabilities
favour Wyat. He was the elder : he had spent
some time in Italy, which Surrey never visited :
and he keeps more closely by the Petrarcan
model, from which the sonnets of Surrey diverge,
and on lines which subsequent Elizabethan
poets steadily widened.*

*For these English experimenters, while con-
stant to the Petrarcan tradition that in substance the sonnet should be a short reflective*

[1] Professor Henry Morley. *English Writers*, vol.
viii. pp. 51-52.

*poem on love, in structure allowed themselves a
licence of innovation which gradually evolved a
type so unlike the Petrarcan that some critics
have believed it a plant of independent growth,
indigenous to our island.*[1] *Others, such as the
late Mr. Mark Pattison, will have nothing to
do with it, and go so far as to declare that the
immortal sonnets of Shakespeare (written on
this model) are "not sonnets at all"!—the aim
of such criticism being apparently the composite
one of vindicating pedantry on the one hand
and saving expense of labour on the other. "If
it had been recognised," says Mr. Pattison,
"that the so-called sonnets of Shakespeare are
not sonnets at all, any more than those of Lord
Brooke, but a continuous poem, or poems, written
in fourteen-line stanzas,* as Tennyson's In
Memoriam *is, largely, in sixteen-line stanzas,
how much misplaced skill would have been
saved!" It is usually possible to save yourself
trouble by considering something as something
else, especially if you thereby remove it from
the category of things you happen to be studying
into the category of things on which you propose
to bestow no attention: but that you serve the*

[1] This theory was advanced by Mr. Hall Caine,
Sonnets of Three Centuries.

interests of sound criticism by this process seems disputable; and yet more disputable when you ignore an author's plain intention. One solid reason (among many) why the Sonnets of Shakespeare are sonnets, while the stanzas of In Memoriam *are not, is that Shakespeare was endeavouring to write sonnets, and Tennyson was endeavouring to do nothing of the sort.*

On the evolution of this Shakespearian type we may say a few words. Wyat observed generally the Petrarcan form in the two opening quatrains (ABBA, ABBA), *and the Petrarcan use of three rhymes in the second part of the sonnet: but he did not observe Petrarch's avoidance of couplets in the second part. He closed every sonnet with a couplet, and this innovation had far-reaching results. Surrey, in the ardour of experiment, attempted many different arrangements of rhyme, but always closed with a couplet; and to this conclusion Spenser was equally loyal. Its expressive value (and it has great expressive value, deny it who will) effaced for a time, in the appreciation of our poets, the more subtly expressive value of the octave and sestet, with their pauses. These vanished as it grew more and more the main business of the sonnet to*

*lead up to a couplet which clinched, as it were,
the thought of the preceding lines with something
of an epigrammatic stroke: until we find the
structure of Surrey's loosest experiments adopted
by Daniel and Shakespeare as the final type of
English sonnet—the easy form of four quatrains
and a couplet all independently rhymed.*

Here are the two forms for comparison:

Petrarcan		Shakespearian	
A		A	
B		B	1
B		A	
A	Octave	B	
A		C	
B		D	2
B		C	Quatrains
A		D	
C		E	
D		F	3
E	Sestet	E	
C		F	
D		G	Couplet
E		G	

*But not even Shakespeare could make the
genius of our language content with this form.*

INTRODUCTION

More learned poets — Ben Jonson in his Sonnet to the Lady Mary Worth, Donne (whose fine Sonnet to Death will be found on p. 75), and Drummond of Hawthornden—soon reverted to the Petrarcan octave for its superior neatness : and Drummond, especially, composed sonnets in large numbers (mostly translations or imitations) which might fairly be called Petrarcan, but for their final couplets. No English writer could yet find it in his heart to end the sonnet otherwise.

Petrarcan in substance it had always remained—an exercise upon the theme of love, usually of hopeless or unsuccessful love : and the theme had fairly exhausted itself in sugared and artificial conceits, when a great poet arose and reformed the English sonnet in substance as well as structure.

Milton—scholar that he was—recognised the beauty of the Petrarcan type and revived its rhyme-arrangement, octave and sestet, with this difference—he obliterated the pauses. A Miltonic sonnet sweeps from opening to close without a break ; it glows " as if he had cut his diamond in such a way that only one luminous light was visible to us" : or again, " he considered—so we may infer—that the English

xiv

sonnet should be like a revolving sphere, every portion becoming continuously visible, with no break in the continuity of thought or expression anywhere apparent." [1] *In one example only—that addressed to Cromwell—did he admit the final couplet. For a true specimen of the noble impetuous Miltonic movement the reader should study the famous " Avenge, O Lord, thy slaughtered saints. . . ."*

But his great and enduring reform was one of substance. To each one of the poets who became colleagues in the Latin Secretaryship under the Protectorate there seems to have come the desire to discover some English vehicle for the Horatian Ode—that singular product so much easier to recognise than describe. Marvel attempted and scored one great success. I refer, of course, to his Horatian Ode *upon Cromwell's* return from Ireland, *and may quote again the often quoted lines on Charles's execution, to exemplify its spirit and its stanzas:*

> *" He nothing common did, or mean,*
> *Upon that memorable scene,*
> *But with his keener eye*
> *The axe's edge did try ;*

---

1 Mr. William Sharp. *The Sonnet,* prefixed to his *Sonnets of This Century.*

INTRODUCTION

> Nor called the gods with vulgar spite
> To vindicate his helpless night;
> But bowed his comely head
> Down as upon a bed."

Though a success, it had no progeny. Milton, steering wider of Horace's Alcaics, chose a verse-form ready to his hand—the Sonnet. "If," says Mr. Robert Bridges,[1] *" we compare, for example, his* Cyriack, whose grandsire, with Martiis cœlebs *or* Æli vetusto, *there can be no doubt that Milton was here deliberately using the sonnet form to do the work of Horace's tight stanzas ; and not the whole of Shakespeare's or Petrarch's sonnets set alongside will show enough kinship with these sonnets of Milton to draw them away from their affinity with Horace."*

But, like many another great artist, Milton carried his experiment to issues far beyond his original aim. His sonnets were no chamber exercises : each owed its inspiration to a real occasion, and that inspiration of reality lifted it high above mere simulation of the Horatian mode. "Each person, thing, or fact is a moment in Milton's life on which he was stirred ; sometimes in the soul's depths, sometimes on the

[1] *Essay on Keats*, printed as a Critical Introduction to the Poems of Keats, edited by G. Thorn Drury

INTRODUCTION

surface of feeling, but always truly moved. . .
It is a man who is speaking to us, not an artist
attitudinising to please us." [1]

>*" In his hand*
>*The Thing became a Trumpet whence he blew*
>*Soul-animating strains——"*

And when, after a slumber of a hundred
years, the sonnet awoke again in England, it
awoke with Milton's seal on its brow. Words-
worth narrates that " in the cottage, Town-end,
Grasmere, one afternoon in 1801, *my sister*
read to me the Sonnets of Milton. I had long
been well acquainted with them, but I was
particularly struck on that occasion with the
dignified simplicity and harmony that runs
through most of them,—in character so differ-
ent from the Italian, and still more so from
Shakespeare's fine Sonnets. I took fire, if I
may be allowed to say so, and produced three
sonnets the same afternoon, the first I ever
wrote except an irregular one at school." [2]

Shakespeare, Milton, Wordsworth, Keats,
Rossetti, Mrs. Browning—these are confessedly
the great sonneteers of our language ; and
though all will not agree in accounting

[1] Mark Pattison.
[2] The irregular sonnet referred to is No. 125 in our
collection. " Calm is all nature as a resting wheel. . ."
Written, perhaps, as early as 1786.

INTRODUCTION

*Wordsworth the greatest, few will deny that
his finest sonnets were harder to spare than
any other's finest. They combine the reality,
the "alive-ness" of Milton's with a more
general and more permanent applicability:
their verity is universal, and appeals to the
conscience of all men. It is given to few to
take more than an historical interest in the
question of parochial endowment and others
which agitated the Long Parliament. Only
the initiated will listen with entire patience
(because with understanding) to the* arcana *of
love as uttered by Shakespeare and Rossetti; or
sympathise with the languors of Keats, or with
the passionate doubts of Mrs. Browning. But
dull indeed would he be of soul who could pass
by such a sonnet as Wordsworth's " The
world is too much with us . . ." or his vale-
dictory sonnet to Duddon, with its immortal
close. " To find," says Mr. John Morley,*[1]
*" beautiful and pathetic language, set to har-
monious numbers, for the common impressions of
meditative minds, is no small part of the poet's
task." It was the part which Wordsworth
performed to perfection. His poetry, as Johnson
said of Gray's Elegy, " abounds with images*

[1] Introduction to the Complete Poetical Works of
William Wordsworth, 1893.

INTRODUCTION

which find a mirror in every mind, and with
sentiments to which every bosom returns an echo."
" I never before," records George Eliot, " met
with so many of my own feelings expressed just
as I should like them."   On the response of the
common conscience of men Wordsworth's sonnets
may rely for their perpetual justification.

   For his form Wordsworth went back to the
true Petrarcan, reintroducing the pause which
Milton had slurred, and reassigning to the
octave and sestet their proper functions.   By the
favour of such artists as Mrs. Browning,
Dante Gabriel Rossetti, Christina Rossetti, Mr.
Swinburne, Mr. William Watson, Mr. Watts-
Dunton, Mr. Gosse, and Mr. Andrew Lang,
and by all but unanimous consent of the critics,
the Petrarcan form has ever since retained its
pride of place.   Keats to be sure (whose sonnets
some lovers of poetry rank next to Shakespeare's;
though on what ground it is hard to see) pro-
vides the dissentients with a sorely needed
support; almost all his early sonnets being
Petrarcan in system and all his later ones
Shakespearian.   But the deliberate reversion
of one poet, even of Keats's quality, cannot
seriously shake the great mass of modern
authority.

xix

INTRODUCTION

It is customary for those who write on this subject to give rules by which a good sonnet may be constructed. But our aim here is not to assist the reader in this or any form of composition. The sonnet has immense popularity just at present, among versifiers. Critics, on the other hand, begin to discover impatience with a form capable of enshrining so much verse of which one can only say, with Charles Lamb, " it discovers much tender feeling; it is most like Petrarch of any foreign Poet, or what we might have supposed Petrarch would have written if Petrarch had been born a fool!" It is hoped that a small volume containing specimens of the best English sonnet-writing of the past will provide the reader with a corrective and a touch-stone of taste. Certainly the study of these specimens ought to assure him that the Sonnet is no arbitrary or haphazard invention; that its length and its peculiar structure were not fixed on by chance; but that every rule has its reason; and that (in a phrase which I may be allowed to repeat) it is the men big enough to break the rules who accept and observe them most cheerfully.

A. T. QUILLER-COUCH.

ENGLISH SONNETS

Sir Thomas Wyat
(1503–1542)

THE LOVER FOR SHAMEFASTNESS HIDETH HIS DESIRE
WITHIN HIS FAITHFUL HEART

THE long Love that in my thought I harbour
   And in my heart doth keep his residence,
   Into my face preaseth with bold pretence,
And there campeth, displaying his banner.
She that me learns to love and to suffer,
   And wills that my trust and lust's negligence
   Be ruled by reason, shame and reverence,
With his hardiness takes displeasure.
Wherewith Love to the heart's forest he fleeth,
   Leaving his enterprise with pain and cry ;
And there him hideth and not appeareth.
What may I do, when my master feareth,
   But in the field with him to live and die?
   For good is the life, ending faithfully.

I

Henry Howard, Earl of Surrey

(1518-1546-7)

DESCRIPTION OF SPRING: WHEREIN EACH THING
RENEWS, SAVE ONLY THE LOVER

THE soote season, that bud and bloom furth
    brings,
    With green hath clad the hill and eke the
      vale,
The nightingale with feathers new she sings;
    The turtle to her mate hath told her tale.
Summer is come, for every spray now springs,
    The hart hath hung his old head on the
      pale;
The buck in brake his winter coat he flings;
    The fishes flete with new repairèd scale;
The adder all her slough away she slings;
    The swift swallow pursueth the flies smale;
The busy bee her honey now she mings;
    Winter is worn that was the flowers' bale.
      And thus I see among these pleasant
        things
      Each care decays, and yet my sorrow
        springs.

HOWARD, EARL OF SURREY

A Vow to Love Faithfully, Howsoever he be
Rewarded

SET me whereas the sun doth parch the green,
　Or where his beams do not dissolve the ice:
In temperate heat, where he is felt and seen ;
　In presence prest of people mad or wise ;
Set me in high, or yet in low degree ;
　In longest night, or in the shortest day ;
In clearest sky, or where clouds thickest be ;
　In lusty youth, or when my hairs are gray :
Set me in heaven, in earth, or else in hell,
　In hill, or dale, or in the foaming flood ;
Thrall, or at large, alive whereso I dwell,
　Sick, or in health, in evil fame, or good,
　　Hers will I be ; and only with this
　　thought
　　Content myself, although my chance be
　　nought.

Earl of Surrey.

SIR EDWARD DYER

Sir Edward Dyer

(*circ.* 1540–1607)

THE SHEPHERD'S CONCEIT OF PROMETHEUS

PROMETHEUS, when first from heaven high
  He brought down fire, ere then on earth
    unseen,
Fond of the light, a satyr, standing by,
  Gave it a kiss, as it like sweet had been.
Feeling forthwith the other's burning power,
  Wood[1] with the smart, with shouts and
    shriekings shrill,
He sought his ease in river, field and bower,
  But for the time his grief went with him still.
So silly I, with that unwonted sight,
  In human shape an angel from above,
Feeding mine eyes, th' impression there did
    light,
  That since I run and rest as pleaseth Love.
    The difference is, the satyr's lips, my
      heart,—
  He for a while, I evermore have smart.

[1] Wild.

4

Sir Walter Raleigh

(1552–1618)

A Vision upon the Faery Queen

METHOUGHT I saw the grave where Laura
lay,
Within that temple where the vestal flame
Was wont to burn; and passing by that way
To see that buried dust of living fame,
Whose tomb fair Love and fairer Virtue kept,
All suddenly I saw the Faery Queen:
At whose approach the soul of Petrarch wept;
And from thenceforth those Graces were not
seen,
For they this Queen attended; in whose stead
Oblivion laid him down on Laura's hearse.
Hereat the hardest stones were seen to bleed,
And groans of buried ghosts the heavens
did pierce,
Where Homer's spright did tremble all
for grief,
And cursed the accéss of that celestial
thief.

5

Edmund Spenser
(1553-1598)

To his Book

HAPPY ye leaves whenas those lily hands,
  Which hold my life in their dead-doing
    might,
Shall handle you, and hold in love's soft bands,
  Like captives trembling at the victor's sight :
  And happy lines, on which with starry light
Those lamping eyes will deign sometime to
    look
  And read the sorrows of my dying sprite,
Written with tears in heart's close bleeding
    book :
  And happy rhymes, bathed in the sacred
    brook
  Of *Helicon*, whence she derivèd is,
When ye behold that angel's blessèd look,
  My soul's long lackèd food, my heaven's
    bliss :
    Leaves, lines, and rhymes, seek her to
    please alone,
    Whom if ye please, I care for other none.

EDMUND SPENSER

RUDELY thou wrongest my dear heart's desire,
  In finding fault with her too portly pride :
The thing which I do most in her admire,
  Is of the world unworthy most envíed ;
  For in those lofty looks is close implied
Scorn of base things, and 'sdeign of foul dis-
    honour,
  Threatening rash eyes which gaze on her so
    wide,
That loosely they ne dare to look upon her.
Such pride is praise, such portliness is honour,
  That boldened innocence bears in her eyes ;
And her fair countenance, like a goodly
    banner,
  Spreads in defiance of all enemies.
    Was never in this world ought worthy
      tried,[1]
    Without some spark of such self-pleasing
      pride.

[1] Proved to be worthy.

EDMUND SPENSER

THE merry Cuckoo, messenger of Spring,
  His trumpet shrill hath thrice already
    sounded ;
That warns all lovers wait upon their king,
  Who now is coming forth with garland
    crownèd.
    With noise whereof the choir of birds re-
      sounded
Their anthems sweet devisèd of Love's praise;
  That all the woods their echoes back re-
    bounded,
As if they knew the meaning of their lays.
But 'mongst them all which did Love's honour
    raise,
  No word was heard of her that most it
    ought :
But she his precept idly disobeys,
  And doth his idle message set at nought.
    Therefore O Love, unless she turn to thee,
    Ere Cuckoo end, let her a rebel be !

EDMUND SPENSER

THIS holy season, fit to fast and pray,
  Men to devotion ought to be inclined :
Therefore I likewise on so holy day
    For my sweet saint some service fit will find.
    Her temple fair is built within my mind,
In which her glorious image placèd is,
    On which my thoughts do day and night
      attend,
Like sacred priests that never think amiss !
There I to her, as the author of my bliss,
  Will build an altar to appease her ire,
And on the same my heart will sacrifice,
    Burning in flames of pure and chaste desire:
    The which vouchsafe O goddess ! to
      accept,
    Amongst thy dearest relics to be kept.

FAIR Proud ! now tell me, why should fair be
    proud ?
  Sith all world's glory is but dross unclean,
And in the shade of death itself shall shroud,
    However now thereof ye little ween !
    That goodly idol, now so gay beseen,
Shall doff her flesh's borrowed fair attire,
    And be forgot as it had never been,
That many now much worship and admire !
Ne any then shall after it inquire,
    Ne any mention shall thereof remain,
But what this verse, that never shall expire,
    Shall to you purchase, with her thankless
      pain.
      Fair ! be no longer proud of that 'shall
      perish ;
      But that which shall you make immortal
      cherish.

EDMUND SPENSER

LIKE as a ship that through the ocean wide,
  By conduct of some star, doth make her way,
Whenas a storm hath dimmed her trusty guide,
  Out of her course doth wander far astray,—
  So I, whose star, that wont with her bright
    ray
Me to direct, with clouds is overcast,
  Do wander now, in darkness and dismay,
Through hidden perils round about me placed;
Yet hope I well that, when this storm is past,
  My Helice, the lodestar of my life,
Will shine again, and look on me at last,
  With lovely light to clear my cloudy grief.
    Till then I wander careful, comfortless,
    In secret sorrow and sad pensiveness.

EDMUND SPENSER

Mark when she smiles with amiable cheer,
  And tell me whereto can ye liken it—
When on each eyelid sweetly do appear
  An hundred Graces as in shade to sit?
  Likest it seemeth to my simple wit
Unto the fair sunshine in summer's day,
  That, when a dreadful storm away is flit,
Through the broad world doth spread his
    goodly ray:
At sight whereof each bird that sits on spray,
  And every beast that to his den was fled,
Comes forth afresh out of their late dismay,
  And to the light lift up their drooping head.
    So my storm-beaten heart likewise is
      cheer'd
    With that sunshine when cloudy looks are
      clear'd.

EDMUND SPENSER

LIKE as a huntsman after weary chase,
 Seeing the game from him escaped away,
Sits down to rest him in some shady place,
 With panting hounds beguilèd of their
  prey :
 So, after long pursuit and vain assay,
When I all weary had the chase forsook,
 The gentle deer returned the self-same way,
Thinking to quench her thirst at the next
  brook.
There she beholding me with milder look,
 Sought not to fly, but fearless still did bide,
Till I in hand her yet half-trembling took,
 And with her own good will her firmly tied.
  Strange things meseemed, to see a beast
   so wild
  So goodly won, with her own will be-
   guiled !

EDMUND SPENSER

Most glorious Lord of life ! that on this day
   Didst make thy triumph over death and sin,
And having harrowed hell didst bring away
   Captivity thence captive, us to win :
   This joyous day, dear Lord, with joy begin;
And grant that we, for whom Thou diddest
    die,
   Being with thy dear blood clean washed from
    sin,
May live for ever in felicity,
And that thy love we weighing worthily,
   May likewise love Thee for the same again ;
And for thy sake, that all like dear didst buy,
   With love may one another entertain.
      So let us love, dear Love, like as we
       ought :
      Love is the lesson which the Lord us
       taught.

EDMUND SPENSER

FRESH Spring, the herald of Love's mighty
    King,
  In whose cote-armour richly are display'd
All sorts of flowers the which on earth do
    spring
  In goodly colours gloriously array'd,—
  Go to my Love, where she is careless laid
Yet in her Winter's bower not well awake :
  Tell her the joyous time will not be stay'd
Unless she do him by the fore-lock take :
Bid her therefore herself soon ready make
  To wait on Love amongst his lovely crew :
Where every one that misseth then her make,[1]
  Shall be by him amerced with penance due.
    Make haste therefore, sweet Love, whilst
      it is prime,
    For none can call again the passèd time.

[1] Mate.

EDMUND SPENSER

ONE day I wrote her name upon the strand,
    But came the waves and washèd it away :
Again I wrote it with a second hand,
    But came the tide and made my pains his
      prey.
    Vain man (said she), that dost in vain assay
A mortal thing so to immortalise ;
    For I myself shall like to this decay,
And eke my name be wiped out likewise.
Not so (quod I) ; let baser things devise
    To die in dust, but you shall live by fame ;
My verse your virtues rare shall eternise,
    And in the heavens write your glorious
      name :
      Where, whenas Death shall all the world
      subdue,
      Our love shall live, and later life renew.

EDMUND SPENSER

LIKE as the Culver [1] on the barèd bough
  Sits mourning for the absence of her mate ;
And in her song sends many a wishful vow
  For his return that seems to linger late.
  So I alone now left disconsolate
Mourn to myself the absence of my love :
  And wand'ring here and there all desolate
Seek with my plaints to match that mournful
    dove.
Ne joy of aught that under heaven doth hove
  Can comfort me, but her own joyous sight
Whose sweet aspect both God and man can
    move
  In her unspotted pleasance to delight.
    Dark is my day whiles her fair light I
    miss,
    And dead my life that wants such lively
    bliss.

                Edmund Spenser.

[1] Dove.

John Florio

(1553-1625)

CONCERNING THE HONOUR OF BOOKS

SINCE honour from the honourer proceeds,
  How well do they deserve that memorize
  And leave in Books for all posterities
The names of worthies and their virtuous
    deeds :
When all their glory else, like water-weeds
  Without their element, presèntly dies,
  And all their greatness quite forgotten lies,
And when and how they flourished no man
    heeds !
How poor remembrances are statues, tombs,
  And other monuments that men erect
To princes, which remain in closèd rooms
  Where but a few behold them, in respect
    Of Books, that to the universal eye
    Show how they lived ; the other where
      they lie !

Sir Philip Sidney

(1554–1586)

WITH how sad steps, O Moon ! thou climb'st
　　the skies !
　How silently, and with how wan a face !
　What ! may it be that even in heavenly
　　place
That busy archer his sharp arrows tries ?
Sure, if that long-with-love-acquainted eyes
　　Can judge of love, thou feel'st a lover's case ;
　　I read it in thy looks : thy languished grace,
To me, that feel the like, thy state descries.
Then, even of fellowship, O Moon ! tell me,
　　Is constant love deemed there but want of
　　　wit ?
Are beauties there as proud as here they be ?
　Do they above love to be loved, and yet
　　Those lovers scorn whom that love doth
　　　possess ?—
　Do they call virtue there ungratefulness ?

Come, Sleep, O Sleep! the certain knot of
peace,
The baiting-place of wit, the balm of woe,
The poor man's wealth, the prisoner's release,
The indifferent judge between the high and
low;
With shield of proof shield me from out the
prease
Of those fierce darts Despair at me doth
throw:
Oh, make in me those civil wars to cease!
I will good tribute pay if thou do so.
Take thou of me smooth pillows, sweetest bed,
A chamber deaf to noise and blind of light,
A rosy garland and a weary head:
And if these things, as being thine by right,
Move not thy heavy grace, thou shalt in
me
Livelier than elsewhere Stella's image see.

SIR PHILIP SIDNEY

Highway! since you my chief Parnassus be,
  And that my Muse, to some ears not un-
    sweet,
  Tempers her words to trampling horses' feet
More oft than to a chamber melody, —
Now blessèd you, bear onward blessèd me
  To her, where I my heart, safe-left, shall
    meet ;
  My Muse and I must you of duty greet,
With thanks and wishes, wishing thankfully.
Be you still fair, honoured by public heed,
  By no encroachment wronged, nor time
    forgot,
Nor blamed for blood, nor shamed for sinful
  deed ;
  And that you know I envy you no lot
    Of highest wish, I wish you so much bliss,
    Hundreds of years you Stella's feet may
      kiss !

SIR PHILIP SIDNEY

My true love hath my heart, and I have his,
  By just exchange one for the other given ;
I hold his dear, and mine he cannot miss ;
  There never was a better bargain driven.
His heart in me keeps me and him in one ;
  My heart in him his thoughts and senses
    guides ;
He loves my heart, for once it was his own ;
  I cherish his because in me it bides.
His heart his wound receivèd from my sight ;
  My heart was wounded with his wounded
    heart :
For as from me on him his hurt did light,
  So still methought in me his hurt did smart.
    Both equal hurt, in this change sought one
      bliss :
    My true love hath my heart, and I have
      his.

SIR PHILIP SIDNEY

Leave me, O Love, which reachest but to
 dust,
 And thou, my mind, aspire to higher things !
Grow rich in that which never taketh rust :
 Whatever fades but fading pleasure brings.
Draw in thy beams, and humble all thy might
 To that sweet yoke where lasting freedoms
 be,
Which breaks the clouds and opens forth the
 light
 That doth both shine and give us sight to
 see.
Oh, take fast hold ! let that light be thy guide
 In this small course which birth draws out
 to death,
And think how evil becometh him to slide
 Who seeketh heaven, and comes of heavenly
 breath.
Then farewell, world ! thy uttermost I see :
Eternal Love, maintain thy life in me !

'Splendidis longum valedico nugis
 Sir Philip Sidney.

Thomas Lodge

(1556?–1625)

O SHADY vales, O fair enrichèd meads,
  O sacred woods, sweet fields, and rising
    mountains ;
O painted flowers, green herbs where Flora
    treads,
  Refresh'd by wanton winds and wat'ry
    fountains !
O all you wingèd choristers of wood,
  That perch'd aloft your former pains report,
And straight again recount with pleasant
    mood
  Your present joys in sweet and seemly sort !
O all you creatures whosoever thrive
  On mother earth, in seas, by air, by fire !—
More blest are you than I here under sun :
Love dies in me, whenas he doth revive
  In you : I perish under beauty's ire,
Where after storms, winds, frosts, your life is
    won.

Robert Greene
(1560-1592)

Ah! were she pitiful as she is fair,
Or but as mild as she is seeming so,
Then were my hopes greater than my despair,
Then all the world were heaven, nothing woe.
Ah! were her heart relenting as her hand,
That seems to melt even with the mildest
touch,
Then knew I where to seat me in a land
Under wide heavens, but yet there is none
such.
So as she shows she seems the budding rose,
Yet sweeter far than is an earthly flower;
Sov'ran of beauty, like the spray she grows;
Compass'd she is with thorns and canker'd
bower.
Yet were she willing to be pluck'd and
worn,
She would be gather'd, though she grew
on thorn.

ℌenry Constable

(1562–1613)

To Sir Philip Sidney's Soul

Give pardon, blessèd soul, to my bold cries,
  If they (importune) interrupt thy song
  Which now, with joyful notes, thou sing'st
    among
The angel-quiristers of heavenly skies ;
Give pardon eke, sweet soul, to my slow cries,
  That since I saw thee now it is so long,
  And yet the tears that unto thee belong
To thee as yet they did not sacrifice.
I did not know that thou wert dead before,
  I did not feel the grief I did sustain :
The greater stroke astonisheth the more,
  Astonishment takes from us sense of pain.
    I stood amazed when others' tears begun,
    And now begin to weep when they have
      done.

HENRY CONSTABLE

To Saint Katharine

BECAUSE thou wast the daughter of a king,
  Whose beauty did all Nature's works exceed,
  And wisdom wonder to the world did breed,
A muse might rouse itself on Cupid's wing;
But, sith the graces which from nature spring
  Were graced by those which from grace did
    proceed,
  And glory have deserved, my Muse doth
    need
An angel's feathers when thy praise I sing.
For all in thee became angelical:
  An angel's face had angels' purity,
And thou an angel's tongue didst speak withal;
    Lo! why thy soul, set free by martyrdom,
  Was crowned by God in angels' company,
    And angels' hands thy body did entomb.
                    Henry Constable.

SAMUEL DANIEL

Samuel Daniel
(1562-1619)

FAIR is my Love, and cruel as she's fair ;
  Her brow shades frowns, although her eyes
    are sunny,
Her smiles are lightning, though her pride
    despair,
  And her disdains are gall, her favours honey:
A modest maid, deck'd with a blush of
    honour,
  Whose feet do tread green paths of youth
    and love ;
The wonder of all eyes that look upon her,
  Sacred on earth, design'd a Saint above.
Chastity and beauty, which were deadly foes,
  Live reconcilèd friends within her brow ;
And had she pity to conjoin with those,
  Then who had heard the plaints I utter now?
    For had she not been fair, and thus un-
      kind,
    My Muse had slept, and none had known
      my mind.

28

SAMUEL DANIEL

My spotless love hovers with purest wings,
    About the temple of the proudest frame,
Where blaze those lights, fairest of earthly
        things,
    Which clear our clouded world with brightest
        flame.
My ambitious thoughts, confinèd in her face ;
    Affect no honour but what She can give ;
My hopes do rest in limits of her grace ;
    I weigh no comfort unless she relieve.
For She, that can my heart unparadise,
    Holds in her fairest hand what dearest is,
My Fortune's wheel's the circle of her eyes,
    Whose rolling grace deign once a turn of
        bliss.
        All my life's sweet consists in her alone ;
        So much I love the most Unloving one.

AND yet I cannot reprehend the flight
  Or blame th' attempt presuming so to soar;
The mounting venture for a high delight
  Did make the honour of the fall the more:
For who gets wealth, that puts not from the
    shore?
  Danger hath honour, great designs their
    fame;
Glory doth follow, courage goes before;
  And though th' event oft answers not the
    same,
Suffice that high attempts have never shame.
  The mean observer, whom base safety keeps
Lives without honour, dies without a name,
  And in eternal darkness ever sleeps:
    And therefore, *Delia*, 'tis to me no blot
    To have attempted, tho' attain'd thee not.

SAMUEL DANIEL

BEAUTY, sweet Love, is like the morning dew,
  Whose short refresh upon the tender green
Cheers for a time, but till the sun doth show ;
  And straight 'tis gone as it had never been.
Soon doth it fade that makes the fairest
      flourish,
  Short is the glory of the blushing rose ;
The hue which thou so carefully dost nourish,
  Yet which at length thou must be forced to
      lose,
When thou, surcharged with burthen of thy
      years,
  Shalt bend thy wrinkles homeward to the
      earth ;
And that, in Beauty's Lease expired, appears
  The Date of Age, the Calends of our Death—
    But ah, no more !—this must not be fore-
      told,
    For women grieve to think they must be
      old.

31

I MUST not grieve my Love, whose eyes would
  read
  Lines of delight, whereon her youth might
  smile ;
Flowers have time before they come to seed,
  And she is young, and now must sport the
  while.
And sport, Sweet Maid, in season of these
  years,
  And learn to gather flowers before they
  wither;
And where the sweetest blossom first appears,
  Let Love and Youth conduct thy pleasures
  thither.
Lighten forth smiles to clear the clouded air,
  And calm the tempest which my sighs do
  raise ;
Pity and smiles do best become the fair ;
  Pity and smiles must only yield the praise.
    Make me to say when all my griefs are
    gone,
    Happy the heart that sighed for such a
    one.

SAMUEL DANIEL

Care-charmer Sleep, son of the sable Night,
  Brother to Death, in silent darkness born,
Relieve my languish and restore the light ;
  With dark forgetting of my care, return :
And let the day be time enough to mourn
  The shipwreck of my ill-adventured youth :
Let waking eyes suffice to wail their scorn,
  Without the torment of the night's untruth.
Cease dreams, the images of day's desires,
  To model forth the passions of the morrow ;
Never let rising Sun approve you liars,
  To add more grief to aggravate my sorrow.
    Still let me sleep, embracing clouds in
      vain,
    And never wake to feel the day's disdain.

SAMUEL DANIEL

LET others sing of Knights and Paladines,
  In aged accents and untimely words,
Paint shadows in imaginary lines,
    Which well the reach of their high wit
    records.
But I must sing of thee, and those fair eyes
  Authentic shall my verse in time to come,
When yet th' unborn shall say, Lo, where she
    lies !
    Whose beauty made him speak, that else
    was dumb !
These are the arcs, the trophies I erect,
  That fortify thy name against old age ;
And these thy sacred virtues must protect
    Against the Dark, and Time's consuming
    rage.
      Though th' error of my youth in them
      appear,
      Suffice, they show I lived, and loved thee
      dear.
Samuel Daniel.

MICHAEL DRAYTON

Michael Drayton

(1563–1613)

CLEAR Anker, on whose silver-sanded shore
  My soul-shrined saint, my fair Idea, lies;
O blessèd brook, whose milk-like swans adore
  Thy crystal stream, refinèd by her eyes!
Where sweet myrrh-breathing Zephyr in the
    spring
  Gently distils his nectar-dropping showers,
Where nightingales in Arden sit and sing
  Amongst the dainty dew-impearlèd flowers;
Say thus, fair brook, when thou shalt see thy
    queen,—
  "Lo, here thy shepherd spent his wandering
    years,
And in these shades, dear nymph, he oft hath
    been,
  And here to thee he sacrificed his tears."
    Fair Arden, thou my Tempe art alone,
    And thou, sweet Anker, art my Helicon.

35

MICHAEL DRAYTON

WHY should your fair eyes with such sovran
    grace
  Disperse their rays on every vulgar spirit,
Whilst I in darkness in the self-same place
  Get not one glance to recompense my merit?
So doth the plowman gaze the wand'ring star,
  And only rest contented with the light,
That never learn'd what constellations are
  Beyond the bent of his unknowing sight.
O why should beauty—custom to obey—
  To their gross sense apply herself so ill?
Would 'God I were as ignorant as they,
  When I am made unhappy by my skill;
    Only compell'd on this poor good to
      boast—
    Heavens are not kind to them that know
      them most.

MICHAEL DRAYTON

Love, banished heaven, in earth was held in
    scorn,
  Wandering abroad in need and beggary,
And wanting friends, though of a goddess
    born,
  Yet craved the alms of such as passèd by ;
I, like a man devout and charitable,
  Clothèd the naked, lodged this wandering
    guest,
With sighs and tears still furnishing his table,
  With what might make the miserable blest.
But this ungrateful, for my good desert,
  Inticed my thoughts against me to conspire,
Who gave consent to steal away my heart,
  And set my breast, his lodging, on a fire.
    Well, well, my friends, when beggars grow
      thus bold,
      No marvel then though charity grow
      cold !

MICHAEL DRAYTON

SINCE there's no help, come let us kiss and
    part,—
    Nay I have done, you get no more of me ;
And I am glad, yea, glad with all my heart,
    That thus so cleanly I myself can free ;
Shake hands for ever, cancel all our vows,
    And when we meet at any time again,
Be it not seen in either of our brows
    That we one jot of former love retain.
Now at the last gasp of Love's latest breath,
    When, his pulse failing, Passion speechless
      lies,
When Faith is kneeling by his bed of death,
    And Innocence is closing up his eyes,—
      Now if thou wouldst, when all have given
        him over,
      From death to life thou mightst him yet
        recover !

                    Michael Drayton.

Charles Best

THE MOON

LOOK how the pale queen of the silent night
  Doth cause the Ocean to attend upon her,
And he, as long as she is in his sight,
  With his full tide is ready her to honour ;
But when the silver waggon of the Moon
  Is mounted up so high he cannot follow,
The sea calls home his crystal waves to moan,
  And with low ebb doth manifest his sorrow.
So you, that are the sovereign of my heart,
  Have all my joys attending on your will,
My joys low-ebbing when you do depart—
  When you return, their tide my heart doth
    fill :
    So as you come, and as you do depart,
    Joys ebb and flow within my tender heart.

THOMAS CAMPION

Thomas Campion

(*ob.* 1620)

THRICE toss these oaken ashes in the air,
  And thrice three times tie up this true-
    love's-knot ;
Thrice sit thee down in this enchanted chair,
  And murmur sóft, "She will, or she will
    not."
Go burn these poisoned weeds in that blue
    fire,
  This cypress gathered at a dead man's grave,
These screech-owl's feathers, and this pricking
    briar,
  That all thy thorny cares an end may have.
Then come, you fairies, dance with me a
    round,
  Dance in this circle, let my Love be centre,
Melodiously breathe out a charming sound,
  Melt her hard heart, that some remorse may
    enter.
    In vain are all the charms I can devise !
    She hath an art to break them with her
      eyes.

40

Joshua Sylvester
(1563–1618)

WERE I as base as is the lowly plain,
  And you, my Love, as high as heaven
    above,
Yet should the thoughts of me, your humble
    swain,
  Ascend to heaven in honour of my Love.
Were I as high as heaven above the plain,
  And you, my Love, as humble and as low
As are the deepest bottoms of the main,
  Wheresoe'er you were, with you my love
    should go.
Were you the earth, dear Love, and I the
    skies,
  My love should shine on you like to the
    Sun,
And look upon you with ten thousand eyes
  Till heaven waxed blind, and till the world
    were done.
    Wheresoe'er I am—below or else above
      you—
    Wheresoe'er you are, my heart shall truly
      love you.

Ignotus

(From *Musica Transalpina.* 1597)

ZEPHYRUS brings the time that sweetly
    scenteth
  With flowers and herbs which winter's frost
    exileth ;
Progne now chirpeth, Philomel lamenteth,
  Flora the garlands white and red compileth ;
Fields do rejoice, the frowning sky relenteth,
  Jove to behold his dearest daughter smileth ;
The air, the water, the earth to joy consenteth,
  Each creature now to love him reconcileth.
But with me, wretch, the storms of woe
    persëver,
  And heavy sighs which from my heart she
    straineth,
That took the key thereof to heaven for ever ;
  So that singing of birds and springtime's
    flow'ring,
And ladies' love that men's affection gaineth,
  Are like a desert and cruel beasts devouring.

William Shakespeare
(1564–1616)

MUSIC to hear, why hear'st thou music sadly?
   Sweets with sweets war not, joy delights in
     joy.
Why lov'st thou that which thou receiv'st not
     gladly,
   Or else receivest with pleasure thine annoy?
If the true concord of well-tuned sounds,
   By unions married, do offend thine ear,
They do but sweetly chide thee, who con-
     founds
   In singleness the parts that thou shouldst
     bear.
Mark how one string, sweet husband to an-
     other,
   Strikes each in each by mutual ordering,
Resembling sire and child and happy mother
   Who all in one, one pleasing note do sing:
     Whose speechless song, being many, seem-
      ing one,
     Sings this to thee: " thou single wilt prove
      none."

43

WILLIAM SHAKESPEARE

When I do count the clock that tells the time,
    And see the brave day sunk in hideous
      night ;
When I behold the violet past prime,
    And sable curls all silver'd o'er with white ;
When lofty trees I see barren of leaves
    Which erst from heat did canopy the herd,
And summer's green all girded up in sheaves
    Borne on the bier with white and bristly
      beard,
Then of thy beauty do I question make,
    That thou among the wastes of time must
      go,
Since sweets and beauties do themselves for-
    sake,
    And die as fast as they see others grow ;
      And nothing 'gainst Time's scythe can
      make defence
    Save breed, to brave him when he takes
      thee hence.

WILLIAM SHAKESPEARE

WHEN to the sessions of sweet silent thought
  I summon up remembrance of things past,
I sigh the lack of many a thing I sought,
  And with old woes new wail my dear time's
    waste ;
Then can I drown an eye, unused to flow,
  For precious friends hid in death's dateless
    night,
And weep afresh love's long since cancell'd
    woe,
  And moan the expense of many a vanish'd
    sight :
Then can I grieve at grievances foregone,
  And heavily from woe to woe tell o'er
The sad account of fore-bemoaned moan,
  Which I now pay as if not paid before.
    But if the while I think on thee, dear
      friend,
    All losses are restored and sorrows end.

THY bosom is endeared with all hearts,
  Which I by lacking have supposed dead,
And there reigns love and all love's loving
    parts,
  And all those friends which I thought buried.
How many a holy and obsequious tear
  Hath dear religious love stol'n from mine
    eye
As interest of the dead, which now appear
  But things removed that hidden in thee lie !
Thou art the grave where buried love doth
    live,
  Hung with the trophies of my lovers gone,
Who all their parts of me to thee did give ;
  That due of many now is thine alone :
    Their images I loved I view in thee,
    And thou, all they, hast all the all of me.

WILLIAM SHAKESPEARE

IF thou survive my well-contented day,
   When that churl Death my bones with dust
      shall cover,
And shalt by fortune once more re-survey
   These poor rude lines of thy deceased lover,
Compare them with the bettering of the time,
   And though they be outstripp'd by every
      pen,
Reserve them for my love, not for their rhyme.
   Exceeded by the height of happier men.
O, then vouchsafe me but this loving thought:
   "Had my friend's Muse grown with this
      growing age,
A dearer birth than this his love had brought,
   To march in ranks of better equipage ;
      But since he died and poets better prove,
      Theirs for their style I'll read, his for his
         love."

FULL many a glorious morning have I seen
  Flatter the mountain-tops with sovereign
    eye,
Kissing with golden face the meadows green,
  Gilding pale streams with heavenly alchemy;
Anon permit the basest clouds to ride
  With ugly rack on his celestial face,
And from the forlorn world his visage hide,
  Stealing unseen to west with this disgrace :
Even so my sun one early morn did shine
  With all-triumphant splendour on my brow ;
But out, alack ! he was but one hour mine ;
  The region cloud had mask'd him from me
    now.
    Yet him for this my love no whit dis-
      daineth;
    Suns of the world may stain when heaven's
      sun staineth.

WILLIAM SHAKESPEARE

So am I as the rich, whose blessed key
   Can bring him to his sweet up-lockèd treasure,
The which he will not every hour survey,
   For blunting the fine point of seldom pleasure.
Therefore are feasts so solemn and so rare,
   Since, seldom coming, in the long year set,
Like stones of worth they thinly placed are,
   Or captain jewels in the carcanet.
So is the time that keeps you as my chest,
   Or as the wardrobe which the robe doth hide,
To make some special instant special blest,
   By new unfolding his imprison'd pride.
      Blessed are you, whose worthiness gives
        scope,
      Being had, to triumph, being lack'd, to
        hope.

WILLIAM SHAKESPEARE

SWEET love, renew thy force ; be it not said
  Thy edge should blunter be than appetite,
Which but to-day by feeding is allay'd,
  To-morrow sharpen'd in his former might :
So, love, be thou ; although to-day thou fill
  Thy hungry eyes even till they wink with
    fulness,
To-morrow see again, and do not kill
  The spirit of love with a perpetual dulness.
Let this sad interim like the ocean be
  Which parts the shore, where two contracted
    new
Come daily to the banks, that, when they see
  Return of love, more blest may be the view ;
    Else call it winter, which being full of care
    Makes summer's welcome thrice more
      wish'd, more rare.

WILLIAM SHAKESPEARE

BEING your slave, what should I do but tend
  Upon the hours and times of your desire?
I have no precious time at all to spend,
  Nor services to do, till you require.
Nor dare I chide the world-without-end hour
  Whilst I, my sovereign, watch the clock for
    you,
Nor think the bitterness of absence sour
  When you have bid your servant once adieu ;
Nor dare I question with my jealous thought
  Where you may be, or your affairs suppose,
But, like a sad slave, stay and think of nought
  Save, where you are how happy you make
    those.
    So true a fool is love that in your Will,
    Though you do any thing, he thinks no ill.

WILLIAM SHAKESPEARE

Like as the waves make towards the pebbled
    shore,
  So do our minutes hasten to their end ;
Each changing place with that which goes
    before,
  In sequent toil all forwards do contend.
Nativity, once in the main of light,
  Crawls to maturity, wherewith being crown'd,
Crooked eclipses 'gainst his glory fight,
  And Time that gave doth now his gift con-
    found.
Time doth transfix the flourish set on youth
  And delves the parallels in beauty's brow,
Feeds on the rarities of Nature's truth,
  And nothing stands but for his scythe to
    mow ;
    And yet to times in hope my verse shall
    stand,
    Praising thy worth, despite his cruel hand.

WILLIAM SHAKESPEARE

WHEN I have seen by Time's fell hand de-
    faced
  The rich proud cost of outworn buried age ;
When sometime lofty towers I see down-razed,
  And brass eternal slave to mortal rage :
When I have seen the hungry ocean gain
  Advantage on the kingdom of the shore,
And the firm soil win of the watery main,
  Increasing store with loss and loss with store ;
When I have seen such interchange of state,
  Or state itself confounded to decay ;
Ruin hath taught me thus to ruminate,
  That time will come and take my love away.
    This thought is as a death, which cannot
      choose
    But weep to have that which it fears to
      lose.

WILLIAM SHAKESPEARE

Since brass, nor stone, nor earth, nor bound-
    less sea,
  But sad mortality o'er-sways their power,
How with this rage shall beauty hold a plea,
  Whose action is no stronger than a flower?
O, how shall summer's honey breath hold out
  Against the wreckful siege of battering days,
When rocks impregnable are not so stout,
    Nor gates of steel so strong, but time de-
    cays?
O fearful meditation! where, alack,
    Shall Time's best jewel from Time's quest
    lie hid?
Or what strong hand can hold his swift foot
    back?
    Or who his spoil of beauty can forbid?
      O, none, unless this miracle have might,
      That in black ink my love may still shine
      bright.

WILLIAM SHAKESPEARE

No longer mourn for me when I am dead
  Than you shall hear the surly sullen bell
Give warning to the world that I am fled
    From this vile world, with vilest worms to
      dwell :
Nay, if you read this line, remember not
  The hand that writ it ; for I love you so
That I in your sweet thoughts would be forgot
  If thinking on me then should make you
    woe.
O, if, I say, you look upon this verse
  When I perhaps compounded am with clay,
Do not so much as my poor name rehearse,
  But let your love even with my life decay,
    Lest the wise world should look into your
      moan
    And mock you with me after I am gone.

WILLIAM SHAKESPEARE

THAT time of year thou mayst in me behold
  When yellow leaves, or none, or few, do
    hang
Upon those boughs which shake against the
  cold,
  Bare ruin'd choirs, where late the sweet
    birds sang.
In me thou see'st the twilight of such day
  As after sunset fadeth in the west,
Which by and by black night doth take away,
  Death's second self, that seals up all in rest.
In me thou see'st the glowing of such fire
  That on the ashes of his youth doth lie,
As the death-bed whereon it must expire
  Consumed with that which it was nourish'd
    by.
    This thou perceivest, which makes thy
      love more strong,
    To love that well which thou must leave
      ere long.

FAREWELL ! thou art too dear for my possess-
  ing,
  And like enough thou know'st thy estimate :
The charter of thy worth gives thee releasing ;
  My bonds in thee are all determinate.
For how do I hold thee but by thy granting?
  And for that riches where is my deserving?
The cause of this fair gift in me is wanting,
  And so my patent back again is swerving.
Thyself thou gavest, thy own worth then not
  knowing,
  Or me, to whom thou gavest it, else mis-
  taking;
So thy great gift, upon misprision growing,
  Comes home again, on better judgment
  making.
    Thus have I had thee as a dream doth
    flatter,
    In sleep a king, but waking no such
    matter.

WILLIAM SHAKESPEARE

THEN hate me when thou wilt; if ever, now;
  Now, while the world is bent my deeds to
    cross,
Join with the spite of fortune, make me bow,
  And do not drop in for an after-loss:
Ah, do not, when my heart hath 'scaped this
    sorrow,
  Come in the rearward of a conquer'd woe:
Give not a windy night a rainy morrow,
  To linger out a purposed overthrow.
If thou wilt leave me, do not leave me last,
  When other petty griefs have done their
    spite,
But in the onset come; so shall I taste
  At first the very worst of fortune's might,
    And other strains of woe, which now seem
      woe,
    Compared with loss of thee will not seem
      so.

WILLIAM SHAKESPEARE

THEY that have power to hurt and will do
    none,
  That do not do the thing they most do show,
Who, moving others, are themselves as stone,
    Unmovèd, cold, and to temptation slow,
They rightly do inherit heaven's graces
    And husband Nature's riches from expense :
They are the lords and owners of their faces,
    Others but stewards of their excellence.
The summer's flower is to the summer sweet,
    Though to itself it only live and die,
But if that flower with base infection meet,
    The basest weed outbraves his dignity :
      For sweetest things turn sourest by their
        deeds ;
      Lilies that fester smell far worse than
        weeds.

WILLIAM SHAKESPEARE

How like a winter hath my absence been
From thee, the pleasure of the fleeting year !
What freezings have I felt, what dark days
seen !
What old December's bareness every where !
And yet this time removed was summer's time,
The teeming autumn, big with rich increase,
Bearing the wanton burden of the prime,
Like widow'd wombs after their lords' de-
cease :
Yet this abundant issue seem'd to me
But hope of orphans and unfather'd fruit ;
For summer and his pleasures wait on thee,
And, thou away, the very birds are mute ;
Or, if they sing, 'tis with so dull a cheer
That leaves look pale, dreading the
winter's near.

WILLIAM SHAKESPEARE

FROM you have I been absent in the spring,
  When proud-pied April dress'd in all his
    trim
Hath put a spirit of youth in every thing,
  That heavy Saturn laugh'd and leap'd with
    him.
Yet nor the lays of birds nor the sweet smell
  Of different flowers in odour and in hue
Could make me any summer's story tell,
  Or from their proud lap pluck them where
    they grew ;
Nor did I wonder at the lily's white,
  Nor praise the deep vermilion in the rose ;
They were but sweet, but figures of delight,
  Drawn after you, you pattern of all those.
    Yet seem'd it winter still, and, you away,
    As with your shadow I with these did
      play.

WILLIAM SHAKESPEARE

THE froward violet thus did I chide :
  Sweet thief, whence didst thou steal thy sweet
    that smells,
If not from my love's breath ?   The purple
  pride
  Which on thy soft cheek for complexion
    dwells
In my love's veins thou hast too grossly dyed.
The lily I condemned for thy hand,
  And buds of marjoram had stol'n thy hair :
The roses fearfully on thorns did stand,
  One blushing shame, another white despair ;
A third, nor red nor white, had stol'n of both,
  And to his robbery had annex'd thy breath ;
But, for his theft, in pride of all his growth
  A vengeful canker eat him up to death.
    More flowers I noted, yet I none could
      see
    But sweet or colour it had stol'n from
      thee.

WILLIAM SHAKESPEARE

My love is strengthen'd, though more weak in
  seeming ;
  I love not less, though less the show appear :
That love is merchandised whose rich esteem-
  ing
    The owner's tongue doth publish every
    where.
Our love was new and then but in the spring,
  When I was wont to greet it with my lays,
As Philomel in summer's front doth sing
  And stops her pipe in growth of riper days :
Not that the summer is less pleasant now
  Than when her mournful hymns did hush
  the night,
But that wild music burthens every bough
  And sweets grown common lose their dear
  delight.
    Therefore like her I sometime hold my
    tongue,
    Because I would not dull you with my
    song.

WILLIAM SHAKESPEARE

To me, fair friend, you never can be old,
  For as you were when first your eye I eyed,
Such seems your beauty still.   Three winters
    cold
    Have from the forests shook three summers'
      pride,
Three beauteous springs to yellow autumn
    turn'd
    In process of the seasons have I seen,
Three April perfumes in three hot Junes burn'd,
  Since first I saw you fresh, which yet are
    green.
Ah ! yet doth beauty, like a dial-hand,
  Steal from his figure and no pace perceived ;
So your sweet hue, which methinks still doth
    stand,
    Hath motion and mine eye may be deceived :
    For fear of which, hear this, thou age
      unbred :
    Ere you were born was beauty's summer
      dead.

WILLIAM SHAKESPEARE

WHEN in the chronicle of wasted time
   I see descriptions of the fairest wights,
And beauty making beautiful old rhyme
   In praise of ladies dead and lovely knights,
Then, in the blazon of sweet beauty's best,
   Of hand, of foot, of lip, of eye, of brow,
I see their antique pen would have express'd
   Even such a beauty as your master now.
So all their praises are but prophecies
   Of this our time, all you prefiguring ;
And, for they look'd but with divining eyes,
     They had not skill enough your worth to
       sing :
     For we, which now behold these present
       days,
     Have eyes to wonder, but lack tongues to
       praise.

WILLIAM SHAKESPEARE

Not mine own fears, nor the prophetic soul
  Of the wide world dreaming on things to
    come,
Can yet the lease of my true love control,
  Supposed as forfeit to a confined doom.
The mortal moon hath her eclipse endured
  And the sad augurs mock their own presage ;
Incertainties now crown themselves assured,
  And peace proclaims olives of endless age.
Now with the drops of this most balmy time
  My love looks fresh, and death to me sub-
    scribes,
Since, spite of him, I'll live in this poor rhyme,
  While he insults o'er dull and speechless
    tribes:
    And thou in this shalt find thy monument,
    When tyrants' crests and tombs of brass
      are spent.

WILLIAM SHAKESPEARE

O, NEVER say that I was false of heart,
   Though absence seem'd my flame to qualify,
As easy might I from myself depart
   As from my soul, which in thy breast doth
     lie :
That is my home of love : if I have ranged,
   Like him that travels I return again,
Just to the time, not with the time exchanged,
   So that myself bring water for my stain.
Never believe, though in my nature reign'd
   All frailties that besiege all kinds of blood,
That it could so preposterously be stain'd,
   To leave for nothing all thy sum of good ;
     For nothing this wide universe I call,
     Save thou, my rose ; in it thou art my all.

WILLIAM SHAKESPEARE

LET me not to the marriage of true minds
   Admit impediments.   Love is not love
Which alters when it alteration finds,
   Or bends with the remover to remove :
O, no ! it is an ever-fixèd mark
   That looks on tempests and is never shaken :
It is the star to every wandering bark,
   Whose worth's unknown, although his height
      be taken.
Love's not Time's fool, though rosy lips and
      cheeks
   Within his bending sickle's compass come ;
Love alters not with his brief hours and weeks,
   But bears it out even to the edge of doom.
     If this be error and upon me proved,
     I never writ, nor no man ever loved.

WILLIAM SHAKESPEARE

The expense of spirit in a waste of shame
  Is lust in action ; and till action, lust
Is perjured, murderous, bloody, full of blame,
  Savage, extreme, rude, cruel, not to trust,
Enjoy'd no sooner but despised straight,
  Past reason hunted, and no sooner had
Past reason hated, as a swallow'd bait
  On purpose laid to make the taker mad ;
Mad in pursuit and in possession so ;
  Had, having, and in quest to have, extreme ;
A bliss in proof, and proved, a very woe ;
  Before, a joy proposed ; behind, a dream.
    All this the world well knows ; yet none
      knows well
    To shun the heaven that leads men to this
      hell.

WILLIAM SHAKESPEARE

Poor soul, the centre of my sinful earth,
   [Sport of] these rebel powers that thee array,
Why dost thou pine within and suffer dearth,
   Painting thy outward walls so costly gay?
Why so large cost, having so short a lease,
   Dost thou upon thy fading mansion spend?
Shall worms, inheritors of this excess,
   Eat up thy charge? is this thy body's end?
Then, soul, live thou upon thy servant's loss,
   And let that pine to aggravate thy store:
Buy terms divine in selling hours of dross;
   Within be fed, without be rich no more:
     So shalt thou feed on Death, that feeds
      on men,
     And Death once dead, there's no more
      dying then.
               William Shakespeare.

Barnaby Barnes
(1568-9–1609)

Ah, sweet Content, where is thy mild abode?
　Is it with shepherds and light-hearted swains
Which sing upon the downs and pipe abroad,
　　Tending their flocks and cattle on the
　　plains?
Ah, sweet Content, where dost thou safely
　　rest?
　　In heaven, with angels which the praises
　　sing
Of Him that made, and rules at His behest,
　The minds and hearts of every living thing?
Ah, sweet Content, where doth thine harbour
　　hold?
　Is it in churches with religious men
Which please the gods with prayers manifold,
　And in their studies meditate it then?—
　　Whether thou dost in heaven or earth
　　appear,
　　Be where thou wilt, thou will not harbour
　　here.

John Davies

(1570–1626)

WHILES in my Soul I feel the soft warm hand
  Of Grace, to thaw the frozen dregs of sin,
She, angel, armed, on Eden's walls doth stand,
    To keep out outward joys that would come
      in ;
But when that holy hand is ta'en away,
  And that my Soul congealeth as before,
She outward comforts seeks with care each
    way,
    And runs to meet them at each sense's door.
Yet they but at the first sight only please,
  Then shrink, or breed abhorred satiety ;
But divine comforts, far unlike to these,
    Do please the more, the more they stay
      and be.
      Then outward joys I inwardly detest,
      Sith they stay not, or stay but in unrest.

John Donne

(1573-1631)

DEATH, be not proud, though some have
called thee
　Mighty and dreadful, for thou art not so ;
　For those whom thou think'st thou dost
　overthrow
Die not, poor Death ; nor yet canst thou kill
me.
From rest and sleep, which but thy pictures
be,
　Much pleasure : then from thee much more
　must flow ;
　And soonest our best men with thee do go—
Rest of their bones and souls' delivery !
Thou'rt slave to fate, chance, kings, and
desperate men,
　And dost with poison, war, and sickness
　dwell ;
　And poppy or charms can make us sleep as
　well,
And better than thy stroke.　Why swell'st
　thou then ?
　　One short sleep past, we wake eternally,
　　And death shall be no more : Death, thou
　　shalt die.

Richard Barnfield
(1574–1627)

To his Friend Maister R. L.

IN PRAISE OF MUSIC AND POETRY

If music and sweet poetry agree,
  As they must needs, the sister and the
    brother,
Then must the love be great 'twixt thee and
    me,
  Because thou lov'st the one, and I the
    other.
Dowland to thee is dear, whose heavenly
    touch
  Upon the lute doth ravish human sense ;
Spenser to me, whose deep conceit is such
  As passing all conceit needs no defence.
Thou lov'st to hear the sweet melodious sound
  That Phœbus' lute, the queen of music,
    makes ;
And I in deep delight am chiefly drowned
  Whenas himself to singing he betakes.
    One god is god of both, as poets feign ;
    One knight loves both, and both in thee
      remain.

76

WILLIAM ALEXANDER

William Alexander, Earl of Stirling
(1580–1640)

OH, if thou knew'st how thou thyself dost
   harm,
  And dost prejudge thy bliss, and spoil my
   rest;
  Then thou wouldst melt the ice out of thy
   breast,
And thy relenting heart would kindly warm.
Oh, if thy pride did not our joys controul,
  What world of loving wonders shouldst thou
   see!
For if I saw thee once transformed in me,
Then in thy bosom I would pour my soul,
Then all thy thoughts should in my visage
   shine;
  And if that ought mischanced, thou shouldst
   not moan
  Nor bear the burthen of thy griefs alone;
No, I would have my share in what were
   thine:
   And whilst we thus should make our
   sorrows one,
   This happy harmony would make them
   none.

77

WILLIAM ALEXANDER

SMALL comfort might my banish'd hopes
  recall
  When 'whiles my dainty fair I sighing see ;
  If I could think that one were shed for me,
It were a guerdon great enough for all :
Or would she let one tear of pity fall
  That seem'd dismiss'd from a remorseful
    eye,
  I could content myself ungrieved to die,
And nothing might my constancy appall.
  The only sound of that sweet word of
    "love,"
Press'd 'twixt those lips that do my doom
  contain,
—Were I embarked—might bring me back
  again
  From death to life, and make me breathe
    and move.
  Strange cruelty ! that never can afford
  So much as once one sigh, one tear, one
    word !
  William Alexander, Earl of Stirling.

78

𝔚illiam 𝔇rummond

(1585-1649)

SLEEP, Silence' child, sweet father of soft rest,
　Prince whose approach peace to all mortal
　　brings,
　Indifferent host to shepherds and to kings,
Sole comforter of minds with grief opprest;
　Lo! by thy charming-rod all breathing
　　things
Lie slumbering, with forgetfulness possest,
　And yet o'er me to spread thy drowsy wings
Thou spares, alas! who cannot be thy guest.
Since I am thine, oh come, but with that face
　To inward light which thou art wont to
　　show;
　With feignèd solace ease a true-felt woe;
Or if, deaf god, thou do deny that grace,
　　Come as thou wilt, and that thou wilt
　　　bequeath,—
　　I long to kiss the image of my death.

ALEXIS, here she stayed ; among these pines,
  Sweet hermitress, she did alone repair ;
  Here did she spread the treasure of her hair,
More rich than that brought from the Colchian
    mines ;
She set her by these muskèd eglantines—
  The happy place the print seems yet to
    bear ;
Her voice did sweeten here thy sugared lines,
  To which winds, trees, beasts, birds, did
    lend their ear ;
Me here she first perceived, and here a morn
  Of bright carnations did o'erspread her face ;
Here did she sigh, here first my hopes were
    born,
  And I first got a pledge of promised grace;
    But ah ! what served it to be happy so,
    Sith passèd pleasures double but new
      woe ?

WILLIAM DRUMMOND

My lute, be as thou wast when thou didst
   grow
   With thy green mother in some shady grove,
   When immelodious winds but made thee
   move,
And birds on thee their ramage [1] did bestow.
   Sith that dear voice which did thy sounds
   approve,
   Which used in such harmonious strains to
   flow,
   Is reft from earth to tune those spheres
   above,
What art thou but a harbinger of woe?
Thy pleasing notes be pleasing notes no more,
   But orphan wailings to the fainting ear;
   Each stop a sigh, each sound draws forth a
   tear;
Be therefore silent as in woods before:
   Or if that any hand to touch thee deign,
   Like widowed turtle still her loss com-
   plain.

   [1] Music of the bough, woodland song.

WILLIAM DRUMMOND

SWEET Spring, thou turn'st with all thy goodly
    train,
  Thy head with flames, thy mantle bright
    with flowers ;
The zephyrs curl the green locks of the plain,
  The clouds for joy in pearls weep down their
    showers :
  Thou turn'st, sweet youth ; but ah ! my
    pleasant hours
And happy days with thee come not again :
The sad memorials only of my pain
  Do with thee turn, which turn my sweets
    in sours.
Thou art the same which still thou wast be-
    fore,
  Delicious, wanton, amiable, fair ;
  But she, whose breath embalmed thy whole-
    some air,
Is gone ; nor gold nor gems her can restore.
    Neglected Virtue ! seasons go and come,
    While thine, forgot, lie closèd in a tomb.

WILLIAM DRUMMOND

WHAT doth it serve to see Sun's burning face,
  And skies enamelled with both Indies' gold?
  Or moon at night in jetty chariot rolled,
And all the glory of that starry place?
  What doth it serve earth's beauty to be-
    hold,—
The mountains' pride, the meadows' flowery
    grace,
  The stately comeliness of forests old,
The sport of floods which would themselves
    embrace?
What doth it serve to hear the sylvans' songs,
  The wanton merle, the nightingale's sad
    strains,
Which in dark shades seem to deplore my
    wrongs?—
  For what doth serve all that this world
    contains?—
  Sith she for whom those once to me were
    dear
  No part of them can have now with me
    here!

WILLIAM DRUMMOND

No Trust in Time

Look how the flower which lingeringly doth
    fade,
    The morning's darling late, the summer's
      queen,
    Spoiled of that juice which kept it fresh and
      green,
As high as it did raise, bows low the head :
Right so my life, contentments being dead,
    Or in their contraries but only seen,
With swifter speed declines than erst it spread,
    And blasted, scarce now shows what it hath
      been.
As doth the pilgrim therefore, whom the
    night
    By darkness would imprison on his way,
Think on thy home, my soul, and think aright
    Of what yet rests thee of life's wasting day !
      Thy sun posts westward, passèd is thy
      morn,
      And twice it is not given thee to be born.

WILLIAM DRUMMOND

The Book of the World

Of this fair volume which we World do name,
  If we the sheets and leaves could turn with
    care,
Of Him who it corrects and did it frame,
  We clear might read the art and wisdom
    rare :
Find out His power which wildest powers doth
    tame,
  His providence extending everywhere,
  His justice which proud rebels doth not
    spare,
In every page, no period of the same.
But silly we, like foolish children, rest
  Well pleased with coloured vellum, leaves
    of gold,
Fair dangling ribbons, leaving what is best,
  On the great writer's sense ne'er taking
    hold ;
    Or if by chance we stay our minds on
      aught,
    It is some picture on the margin wrought.

WILLIAM DRUMMOND

The last and greatest herald of heaven's King,
   Girt with rough skins, hies to the deserts
      wild,
Among that savage brood the woods forth
      bring,
   Which he than man more harmless found
      and mild.
His food was locusts, and what there doth
      spring,
   With honey that from virgin hives distilled ;
Parcht body, hollow eyes, some uncouth
      thing
   Made him appear, long since from earth
      exiled.
There burst he forth : All ye whose hopes
      rely
   On God, with me amidst these deserts
      mourn,
Repent, repent, and from old errors turn !—
Who listened to his voice, obeyed his cry ?
   Only the echoes, which he made relent,
      Rung from their flinty caves, Repent !
         Repent !

WILLIAM DRUMMOND

The Magdalen

THESE eyes, dear Lord! once brandons of
    desire,
  Frail scouts betraying what they had to
    keep,
Which their own heart, then others set on fire,
  Their traitrous black before Thee here out-
    weep :
These locks, of blushing deeds the fair attire,
  Smooth-frizzled waves, sad shelves which
    shadow deep,
  Soul-stinging serpents in gilt curls which
    creep,
To touch Thy sacred feet do now aspire.
In seas of care behold a sinking bark,
  By winds of sharp remorse unto Thee
    driven ;
Oh, let me not exposed be ruin's mark !
  My faults confest—Lord, say they are for-
    given !
  Thus sighed to Jesus the Bethanian fair,
  His tear-wet feet still drying with her
    hair.

WILLIAM DRUMMOND

To a Nightingale

Sweet bird, that sing'st away the early hours,
  Of winters past or coming void of care,
  Well pleasèd with delights which present
    are,
Fair seasons, budding sprays, sweet-smelling
    flowers;
To rocks, to springs, to rills, from leafy
    bowers
  Thou thy Creator's goodness dost declare,
  And what dear gifts on thee He did not
    spare,
A stain to human sense in sin that lowers.
What soul can be so sick which by thy songs,
  Attired in sweetness, sweetly is not driven
Quite to forget earth's turmoils, spites, and
    wrongs,
  And lift a reverend eye and thought to
    heaven!
    Sweet artless songster, thou my mind dost
    raise
    To airs of spheres, yes, and to angels'
    lays.

WILLIAM DRUMMOND

As when it happeneth that some lovely town
  Unto a barbarous besieger falls,
  Who there by sword and flame himself in-
    stalls,
And, cruel, it in tears and blood doth drown ;
  Her beauty spoiled, her citizens made thralls,
His spite yet so can not her all throw down
But that some statue, arch, fane of renown
  Yet lurks unmaimed within her weeping
    walls :
So, after all the spoil, disgrace, and wrack,
  That time, the world, and death, could
    bring combined,
Amidst that mass of ruins they did make,
  Safe and all scarless yet remains my mind.
    From this so high transcending rapture
      springs,
    That I, all else defaced, not envy kings.
                              William Drummond.

89

William Browne of Tavistock

(1590–1645)

A ROSE, as fair as ever saw the north,
  Grew in a little garden all alone :
A sweeter flower did Nature ne'er put forth,
  Nor fairer garden yet was never known.
The maidens danced about it morn and noon,
  And learnèd bards of it their ditties made ;
The nimble fairies, by the pale-faced moon,
  Watered the root, and kissed her pretty
    shade.
But, welladay ! the gardener careless grew,
  The maids and fairies both were kept away,
And in a drought the caterpillars threw
  Themselves upon the bud and every spray.
    God shield the stock !   If heaven send no
      supplies,
    The fairest blossom of the garden dies.

George Herbert

(1593-1632)

SIN

LORD, with what care hast Thou begirt us
    round!
Parents first season us; then schoolmasters
Deliver us to laws; they send us bound
    To rules of reason, holy messengers,
Pulpits and Sundays, sorrow dogging sin,
    Afflictions sorted, anguish of all sizes,
Fine nets and stratagems to catch us in,
    Bibles laid open, millions of surprises;
Blessings beforehand, ties of gratefulness,
    The sound of glory ringing in our ears;
Without, our shame; within, our consciences;
    Angels and grace, eternal hopes and fears.
        Yet all these fences and their whole array
        One cunning bosom-sin blows quite away.

William Habington

(1605–1645)

LOVE'S ANNIVERSARY
TO THE SUN

THOU art returned, great light, to that blest
  hour
In which I first by marriage, sacred power,
    Joined with Castara hearts : and as the same
    Thy lustre is, as then, so is our flame ;
Which had increased, but that by love's decree
'Twas such at first it ne'er could greater be.
    But tell me, glorious lamp, in thy survey
    Of things below thee, what did not decay
By age to weakness ?—I since that have seen
The rose bud forth and fade, the tree grow
    green
    And wither, and the beauty of the field
    With winter wrinkled.   Even thyself dost
      yield
      Something to time, and to thy grave fall
      nigher ;—
      But virtuous love is one sweet endless
      fire.

John Milton

(1608–1674)

To the Nightingale

O NIGHTINGALE ! that on yon bloomy spray
  Warblest at eve, when all the woods are
    still,
  Thou with fresh hope the lover's heart
    dost fill,
While the jolly hours lead on propitious May.
Thy liquid notes that close the eye of day,
  First heard before the shallow cuckoo's bill,
  Portend success in love.   O, if Jove's will
Have linked that amorous power to thy soft
    lay,
Now timely sing, ere the rude bird of hate
  Foretell my hopeless doom, in some grove
    nigh ;
As thou from year to year hast sung too late
  For my relief, yet hadst no reason why.
Whether the Muse or Love call thee his mate,
  Both them I serve, and of their train am I.

JOHN MILTON

On his having Arrived at the Age of Twenty-three

How soon hath Time, the subtle thief of youth,
  Stolen on his wing my three-and-twentieth
    year !
  My hasting days fly on with full career,
But my late spring no bud or blossom
    shew'th.
Perhaps my semblance might deceive the truth
  That I to manhood am arrived so near ;
  And inward ripeness doth much less appear,
That some more timely happy spirits indu'th.
Yet, be it less or more, or soon or slow,
  It shall be still in strictest measure even
    To that same lot, however mean or high,
    Toward which Time leads me, and the will
      of Heaven.
All is, if I have grace to use it so,
    As ever in my great Taskmaster's eye.

JOHN MILTON

CAPTAIN or Colonel, or Knight in Arms,
   Whose chance on these defenceless doors
     may seize,
   If deed of honour did thee ever please,
Guard them, and him within protect from
     harms.
He can requite thee; for he knows the charms
   That call fame on such gentle acts as
     these,
   And he can spread thy name o'er lands
     and seas,
Whatever clime the sun's bright circle warms.
Lift not thy spear against the Muses' bower:
   The great Emathian conqueror bid spare
The house of Pindarus, when temple and
     tower
   Went to the ground; and the repeated air
Of sad Electra's poet had the power
   To save the Athenian walls from ruin bare.

95

JOHN MILTON

Lady, that in the prime of earliest youth
  Wisely hast shunned the broad way and
    the green,
  And with those few art eminently seen
That labour up the hill of heavenly Truth,
The better part with Mary and with Ruth
  Chosen thou hast; and they that over-
    ween,
  And at thy growing virtues fret their spleen,
No anger find in thee, but pity and ruth.
Thy care is fixed, and zealously attends
    To fill thy odorous lamp with deeds of
      light,
      And hope that reaps not shame. There-
      fore be sure
Thou, when the Bridegroom with his feastful
    friends
  Passes to bliss at the mid-hour of night,
    Hast gained thy entrance, virgin wise
      and pure.

JOHN MILTON

DAUGHTER to that good Earl, once President
  Of England's Council and her Treasury,
    Who lived in both unstained with gold or
      fee,
And left them both, more in himself content,
Till the sad breaking of that Parliament
  Broke him, as that dishonest victory
    At Chæronea, fatal to liberty,
Killed with report that old man eloquent,
Though later born than to have known the
    days
  Wherein your father flourished, yet by
    you,
    Madam, methinks I see him living yet :
So well your words his noble virtues praise
  That all both judge you to relate them
    true
    And to possess them, honoured Margaret.

JOHN MILTON

To Mr. H. Lawes on his Airs

Harry, whose tuneful and well-measured song
  First taught our English music how to
    span
  Words with just note and accent, not to
    scan
With Midas' ears, committing short and long,
Thy worth and skill exempts thee from the
    throng,
  With praise enough for Envy to look wan ;
  To after age thou shalt be writ the man
That with smooth air couldst humour best our
    tongue.
Thou honour'st Verse, and Verse must send
    her wing
  To honour thee, the priest of Phœbus'
    quire,
    That tunest their happiest lines in hymn
    or story.
  Dante shall give Fame leave to set thee
    higher
Than his Casella, whom he wooed to sing,
    Met in the milder shades of Purgatory.

JOHN MILTON

On the Religious Memory of Mrs. Catherine
Thomson, my Christian Friend, deceased
Dec. 16, 1646

When Faith and Love, which parted from
    thee never,
    Had ripened thy just soul to dwell with
    God,
    Meekly thou didst resign this earthy load
Of death, called life, which us from life doth
    sever.
Thy works, and alms, and all thy good en-
    deavour,
    Stayed not behind, nor in the grave were
    trod ;
    But, as Faith pointed with her golden rod,
Followed thee up to joy and bliss for ever
Love led them on ; and Faith, who knew them
    best
    Thy handmaids, clad them o'er with purple
    beams
And azure wings, that up they flew so drest,
    And speak the truth of thee on glorious
    themes
Before the Judge ; who thenceforth bid thee
    rest,
    And drink thy fill of pure immortal streams.

JOHN MILTON

To the Lord General Cromwell, May 1652

ON THE PROPOSALS OF CERTAIN MINISTERS AT THE
COMMITTEE FOR PROPAGATION OF THE GOSPEL

CROMWELL, our chief of men, who through a
    cloud
  Not of war only, but detractions rude,
  Guided by faith and matchless fortitude,
To peace and truth thy glorious way hast
    ploughed,
And on the neck of crowned Fortune proud
  Hast reared God's trophies, and His work
    pursued,
  While Darwen stream, with blood of Scots
    imbrued,
And Dunbar field, resounds thy praises loud,
And Worcester's laureate wreath : yet much
    remains
  To conquer still ; Peace hath her victories
  No less renowned than War : new foes arise,
Threatening to bind our souls with secular
    chains.
    Help us to save free conscience from the
    paw
    Of hireling wolves, whose Gospel is their
    maw.

JOHN MILTON

Vane, young in years, but in sage counsel
    old,
    Than whom a better senator ne'er held
    The helm of Rome, when gowns, not arms,
    repelled
The fierce Epirot and the African bold,
Whether to settle peace, or to unfold
    The drift of hollow states hard to be spelled;
    Then to advise how war may, best upheld,
Move by her two main nerves, iron and gold,
In all her equipage; besides, to know
    Both spiritual power and civil, what each
        means,
        What severs each, thou hast learned, which
        few have done.
The bounds of either sword to thee we owe:
    Therefore on thy firm hand Religion leans
        In peace, and reckons thee her eldest son.

JOHN MILTON

ON THE LATE MASSACRE IN PIEDMONT

AVENGE, O Lord, thy slaughtered saints, whose bones
   Lie scattered on the Alpine mountains cold ;
   Even them who kept Thy truth so pure of old,
When all our fathers worshipped stocks and stones,
Forget not : in Thy book record their groans
   Who were Thy sheep, and in their ancient fold
   Slain by the bloody Piemontese, that rolled
Mother with infant down the rocks. Their moans
The vales redoubled to the hills, and they
   To heaven. Their martyred blood and ashes sow
O'er all the Italian fields, where still doth sway
   The triple Tyrant ; that from these may grow
A hundredfold, who, having learnt Thy way,
Early may fly the Babylonian woe.

JOHN MILTON

On his Blindness

WHEN I consider how my light is spent
  Ere half my days in this dark world and
    wide,
  And that one talent which is death to hide
Lodged with me useless, though my soul more
    bent
To serve therewith my Maker, and present
  My true account, lest He, returning, chide,
  "Doth God exact day-labour, light denied?"
I fondly ask. But Patience, to prevent
That murmur, soon replies, "God doth not
    need
  Either man's work or his own gifts. Who
    best
  Bear His mild yoke, they serve Him best.
    His state
Is kingly : thousands at His bidding speed,
  And post o'er land and ocean without rest;
  They also serve who only stand and wait."

JOHN MILTON

To Mr. Lawrence

LAWRENCE, of virtuous father virtuous son,
   Now that the fields are dank, and ways
     are mire,
   Where shall we sometimes meet, and by
     the fire
Help waste a sullen day, what may be won
   From the hard season gaining? Time will
     run
   On smoother, till Favonius reinspire
   The frozen earth, and clothe in fresh attire
The lily and rose, that neither sowed nor spun.
What neat repast shall feast us, light and
     choice,
   Of Attic taste, with wine, whence we may
     rise
To hear the lute well touched, or artful voice
   Warble immortal notes and Tuscan air?
   He who of those delights can judge, and
     spare
To interpose them oft, is not unwise.

JOHN MILTON

CYRIACK, whose grandsire on the royal bench
  Of British Themis, with no mean applause,
  Pronounced, and in his volumes taught,
      our laws,
Which others at their bar so often wrench,
To-day deep thoughts resolve with me to
      drench
  In mirth that after no repenting draws ;
  Let Euclid rest, and Archimedes pause,
And what the Swede intend, and what the
      French.
To measure life learn thou betimes, and know
  Toward solid good what leads the nearest
        way ;
      For other things mild Heaven a time
        ordains,
And disapproves that care, though wise in
    show,
  That with superfluous burden loads the day,
    And, when God sends a cheerful hour,
      refrains.

105

JOHN MILTON

CYRIACK, this three years' day these eyes, though clear,
  To outward view, of blemish or of spot,
  Bereft of light, their seeing have forgot ;
Nor to their idle orbs doth sight appear
Of sun, or moon, or star, throughout the year,
  Or man, or woman.   Yet I argue not
  Against Heaven's hand or will, nor bate a jot
Of heart or hope, but still bear up and steer
Right onward.   What supports me, dost thou ask ?
  The conscience, friend, to have lost them overplied
In Liberty's defence, my noble task,
  Of which all Europe rings from side to side.
This thought might lead me through the world's vain mask
  Content, though blind, had I no better guide.

JOHN MILTON

METHOUGHT I saw my late espoused saint
   Brought to me like Alcestis from the grave,
   Whom Jove's great son to her glad husband
      gave,
Rescued from Death by force, though pale and
      faint.
Mine, as whom washed from spot of child-bed
      taint
   Purification in the Old Law did save,
   And such as yet once more I trust to have
Full sight of her in Heaven without restraint,
Came vested all in white, pure as her mind.
   Her face was veiled; yet to my fancied
      sight
Love, sweetness, goodness, in her person
      shined
   So clear as in no face with more delight.
But, oh! as to embrace me she inclined,
   I waked, she fled, and day brought back my
      night.

                John Milton.

Thomas Edwards

(1699–1757)

To Richard Owen Cambridge

CAMBRIDGE, with whom, my pilot and my
    guide,
  Pleased I have traversed thy Sabrina's flood,
  Both where she foams impetuous, soiled
    with mud,
And where she peaceful rolls her golden tide ;
Never, oh, never let ambition's pride
  (Too oft pretexèd with our country's good),
  And tinselled pomp, despised when under-
    stood,
Or thirst of wealth, thee from her banks
    divide !
Reflect how calmly, like her infant wave,
  Flows the clear current of a private life ;
    See the wide public stream, by tempests
      tost,
Of every changing wind the sport or slave,
  Soiled with corruption, vexed with party
    strife,
    Covered with wrecks of peace and honour
      lost.

Thomas Gray

(1706–1771)

ON THE DEATH OF RICHARD WEST

IN vain to me the smiling mornings shine,
  And reddening Phœbus lifts his golden fire ;
The birds in vain their amorous descant join,
  Or cheerful fields resume their green attire :
These ears, alas ! for other notes repine,
  A different object do these eyes require ;
My lonely anguish melts no heart but mine,
  And in my breast the imperfect joys expire.
Yet morning smiles the busy race to cheer,
  And new-born pleasure brings to happier
    men ;
The fields to all their wonted tribute bear,
  To warm their little loves the birds com-
    plain :
I fruitless mourn to him that cannot hear,
  And weep the more because I weep in vain.

William Mason

(1725–1797)

ANNIVERSARY. FEB. 23, 1795

A PLAINTIVE sonnet flowed from Milton's pen
When Time had stolen his three-and-twen-
    tieth year :
  Say, shall not I then shed one tuneful tear,
Robbed by the thief of three-score years and
    ten?
No ! for the foes of all life-lengthened men,
  Trouble and toil, approach not yet too near ;
  Reason, meanwhile, and health, and memory
    dear
Hold unimpaired their weak yet wonted
    reign :
Still round my sheltered lawn I pleased can
    stray ;
  Still trace my sylvan blessings to their
    spring :
BEING of BEINGS ! yes, that silent lay
  Which musing Gratitude delights to sing,
Still to thy sapphire throne shall Faith convey,
  And Hope, the cherub of unwearied wing.

Thomas Warton
(1728–1790)

WHEN late the trees were stript by Winter
  pale,
 Young Health, a dryad-maid in vesture
  green,
 Or like the forest's silver-quiver'd queen,
On airy uplands met the piercing gale ;
And, ere its earliest echo shook the vale,
 Watching the hunter's joyous horn was seen.
 But since, gay-thron'd in fiery chariot sheen,
Summer has smote each daisy-dappled dale,
She to the cave retires, high-arched beneath
 The fount that laves proud Isis' towery
  brim ;
And now all glad the temperate air to
  breathe,
 While cooling drops distil from arches
  dim,
Binding her dewy locks with sedgy wreath
 She sits amid the quire of Naiads trim.

III

THOMAS WARTON

Deem not devoid of elegance the sage,
  By Fancy's genuine feelings unbeguiled,
  Of painful pedantry the poring child,
Who turns of these proud domes the historic
      page,
Now sunk by Time and Henry's fiercer rage.
  Think'st thou the warbling Muses never
      smiled
On his lone hours? Ingenuous views engage
  His thoughts, on themes, unclassic falsely
      styled,
Intent. While cloistered Piety displays
  Her mouldering roll, the piercing eye ex-
      plores
New manners, and the pomp of elder days,
  Whence culls the pensive bard his pictured
      stores.
Nor rough nor barren are the winding ways
  Of hoar Antiquity, but strewn with flowers.

THOMAS WARTON

AH ! what a weary race my feet have run,
  Since first I trod thy banks with alders
    crowned,
  And thought my way was all through fairy
    ground,
Beneath thy azure sky and golden sun :
Where first my Muse to lisp her notes begun !
  While pensive Memory traces back the
    round
Which fills the varied interval between ;
Much pleasure, more of sorrow, marks the
    scene.
Sweet native stream ! those skies and suns so
    pure
  No more return, to cheer my evening road !
Yet still one joy remains,—that not obscure,
  Nor useless, all my vacant days have flowed,
From youth's gay dawn to manhood's prime
    mature ;
  Nor with the Muse's laurel unbestowed.

Thomas Warton.

William Cowper

(1731–1800)

To Henry Cowper, on his Defence of Warren Hastings in the House of Lords

Cowper, whose silver voice, task'd sometimes
    hard
   Legends prolix delivers in the ears
   (Attentive when thou read'st) of England's
    peers,
Let verse at length yield thee thy just reward.
Thou wast not heard with drowsy disregard,
   Expending late on all that length of plea
   Thy generous pow'rs ; but silence honoured
    thee,
Mute as e'er gazed on orator or bard.
Thou art not voice alone ; but hast beside
   Both heart and head ; and couldst with
     music sweet
   Of Attic phrase and senatorial tone,
Like thy renown'd forefathers, far and wide
   Thy fame diffuse, praised not for utterance
    meet
    Of other's speech, but magic of thy own.

114

WILLIAM COWPER

TO MRS. UNWIN

MARY! I want a lyre with other strings,
  Such aid from heaven as some have feigned
    they drew,
  An eloquence scarce given to mortals, new
And undebased by praise of meaner things ;
That, ere through age or woe I shed my wings,
  I may record thy worth with honour due,
  In verse as musical as thou art true,
And that immortalizes whom it sings.
But thou hast little need.   There is a Book
  By seraphs writ with beams of heavenly
    light,
On which the eyes of God not rarely look,
  A chronicle of actions just and bright ;—
    There all thy deeds, my faithful Mary,
      shine ;
    And since thou own'st that praise, I spare
      thee mine.
                William Cowper.

Anna Seward

(1747–1809)

December Morning

I LOVE to rise ere gleams the tardy light,
  Winter's pale dawn ; and as warm fires
    illume,
  And cheerful tapers shine around the room,
Through misty windows bend my musing sight,
Where, round the dusky lawn, the mansions
    white,
    With shutters closed, peer faintly through
      the gloom
    That slow recedes ; while yon grey spires
      assume,
Rising from their dark pile, an added height
By indistinctness given.—Then to decree
  The grateful thoughts to God, ere they un-
    fold
To friendship or the Muse, or seek with glee
  Wisdom's rich page. O hours more worth
    than gold,
By whose blest use we lengthen life, and, free
  From drear decays of age, outlive the old !

Charlotte Smith

(1749–1806)

SWEET poet of the woods, a long adieu!
　Farewell, soft minstrel of the early year!
Ah! 'twill be long ere thou shalt sing anew,
　And pour thy music on the night's dull ear.
Whether on spring thy wandering flights
　　await,
　Or whether silent in our groves you dwell,
The pensive Muse shall own you for her mate,
　And still protect the song she loves so well.
With cautious step the lovelorn youth shall
　　glide
　Thro' the lone glade that shades thy mossy
　　nest,
And shepherd-girls from eyes profane shall
　　hide
　The gentle bird who sings of pity best;
　　For still thy voice shall soft affections
　　　move,
　　And still be dear to sorrow and to love.

John Codrington Bamfylde

(1754–1796)

On a wet Summer

ALL ye who far from town in rural hall,
  Like me, were wont to dwell near pleasant
    field,
  Enjoying all the sunny day did yield,
With me the change lament, in irksome thrall,
By rains incessant held; for now no call
  From early swain invites my hand to wield
  The scythe. In parlour dim I sit concealed,
And mark the lessening sand from hour-glass
    fall;
Or 'neath my window view the wistful train
  Of dripping poultry, whom the vine's broad
    leaves
Shelter no more. Mute is the mournful plain;
  Silent the swallow sits beneath the thatch,
  And vacant hind hangs pensive o'er his
    hatch,
  Counting the frequent drips from reeded
    eaves.

118

THOMAS RUSSELL

Thomas Russell
(1762–1788)

SUPPOSED TO BE WRITTEN AT LEMNOS

ON this lone isle, whose rugged rocks affright
  The cautious pilot, ten revolving years
  Great Pæan's son, unwonted erst to tears,
Wept o'er his wound : alike each rolling light
Of heaven he watched, and blamed its linger-
    ing flight;
  By day the sea-mew screaming round his
    cave
  Drove slumber from his eyes; the chiding
    wave
And savage howlings chased his dreams by
    night.
Hope still was his : in each low breeze that
    sighed
  Through his rude grot he heard a coming
    oar,
In each white cloud a coming sail he spied;
  Nor seldom listened to the fancied roar
Of Œta's torrents, or the hoarser tide
  That parts famed Trachis from the Euboic
    shore.

Ibelen Maria Williams

(1762–1828)

To Hope

O EVER skilled to wear the form we love !
  To bid the shapes of fear and grief depart ;
Come, gentle Hope ! with one gay smile remove
  The lasting sadness of an aching heart.
Thy voice, benign enchantress ! let me hear ;
  Say that for me some pleasures yet shall
    bloom,—
That fancy's radiance, friendship's precious
    tear,
  Shall soften, or shall chase, misfortune's
    gloom.
But come not glowing in the dazzling ray
  Which once with dear illusions charmed my
    eye ;
Oh, strew no more, sweet flatterer ! on my
    way
  The flowers I fondly thought too bright to
    die :
  Visions less fair will soothe my pensive
    breast,
  That asks not happiness, but longs for
    rest.

Sir Samuel Egerton Brydges
(1762–1837)

ON ECHO AND SILENCE

IN eddying course when leaves began to fly,
  And Autumn in her lap the store to strew,
    As 'mid wild scenes I chanced the Muse to
      woo,
Through glens untrod and woods that frowned
  on high,
Two sleeping nymphs with wonder mute I
  spy !—
    And lo, she's gone !—in robe of dark green
    hue,
  'Twas Echo from her sister Silence flew :
For quick the hunter's horn resounded to the
  sky !
In shade affrighted Silence melts away.
  Not so her sister !—hark, for onward still
With far-heard step she takes her listening
  way,
    Bounding from rock to rock, and hill to
    hill !
Ah, mark the merry maid in mockful play
  With thousand mimic tones the laughing
    forest fill.

William Lisle Bowles

(1762–1850)

OSTEND

ON HEARING THE BELLS AT SEA

How sweet the tuneful bells' responsive peal!
  As when at opening dawn the fragrant
    breeze
Touches the trembling sense of pale disease,
So piercing to my heart their force I feel.
  And hark! with lessening cadence now
    they fall,
And now along the white and level tide
They fling their melancholy music wide;
  Bidding me many a tender thought recall
Of summer days, and those delightful years
  When by my native streams, in life's fair
    prime,
  The mournful magic of their mingling
    chime
First waked my wondering childhood into
    tears!
    But seeming now, when all those days
      are o'er,
    The sounds of joy once heard and heard
      no more.

WILLIAM LISLE BOWLES

O TIME ! who know'st a lenient hand to lay
  Softest on sorrow's wound, and slowly
    thence,
  Lulling to sad repose the weary sense,
The faint pang stealest unperceived away ;
  On thee I rest my only hope at last,
And think, when thou hast dried the bitter
     tear
That flows in vain o'er all my soul held dear,
  I may look back on every sorrow past,
And meet life's peaceful evening with a smile;—
  As some lone bird, at day's departing hour,
  Sings in the sunbeam, of the transient
    shower
Forgetful, though its wings are wet the
    while :—
    Yet, ah ! how much must that poor heart
     endure,
    Which hopes from thee, and thee alone, a
     cure !

               W. L. Bowles.

William Wordsworth

(1770–1850)

Nuns fret not at their convent's narrow room ;
 And hermits are contented with their cells ;
 And students with their pensive citadels :
Maids at the wheel, the weaver at his loom,
Sit blithe and happy ; bees that soar for bloom,
 High as the highest peak of Furness Fells,
 Will murmur by the hour in foxglove bells :
In truth the prison unto which we doom
Ourselves, no prison is : and hence for me,
 In sundry moods, 'twas pastime to be bound
 Within the sonnet's scanty plot of ground :
Pleased if some souls (for such there needs
  must be)
Who have felt the weight of too much liberty,
 Should find brief solace there, as I have
  found.

WILLIAM WORDSWORTH

CALM is all nature as a resting wheel.
　The kine are couched upon the dewy grass ;
　The horse alone, seen dimly as I pass,
Is cropping audibly his later meal :
Dark is the ground ; a slumber seems to steal
　O'er vale, and mountain, and the starless
　　sky.
　Now, in this blank of things, a harmony,
Home-felt, and home-created, seems to heal
　That grief for which the senses still supply
　Fresh food ; for only then, when memory
Is hushed, am I at rest.　My friends ! restrain
Those busy cares that would allay my pain :
　Oh ! leave me to myself ; nor let me feel
The officious touch that makes me droop again.

WILLIAM WORDSWORTH

Composed upon Westminster Bridge, September 3, 1802

EARTH has not anything to show more fair:
  Dull would he be of soul who could pass by
  A sight so touching in its majesty:
This City now doth, like a garment, wear
The beauty of the morning ; silent, bare,
  Ships, towers, domes, theatres, and temples
    lie
  Open unto the fields, and to the sky;
All bright and glittering in the smokeless air.
Never did sun more beautifully steep
  In his first splendour, valley, rock, or hill ;
Ne'er saw I, never felt, a calm so deep !
  The river glideth at his own sweet will :
Dear God ! the very houses seem asleep ;
  And all that mighty heart is lying still !

WILLIAM WORDSWORTH

IT is a beauteous Evening, calm and free,
  The holy time is quiet as a Nun
  Breathless with adoration ; the broad sun
Is sinking down in its tranquillity ;
The gentleness of heaven broods o'er the Sea;
  Listen ! the mighty Being is awake,
  And doth with his eternal motion make
A sound like thunder—everlastingly.
Dear Child ! dear Girl ! that walkest with me
      here,
  If thou appear untouched by solemn thought,
    Thy nature is not therefore less divine ;
Thou liest in Abraham's bosom all the year ;
    And worship'st at the Temple's inner
      shrine,
  God being with thee when we know it not.

WILLIAM WORDSWORTH

Once did She hold the gorgeous East in fee ;
    And was the safeguard of the West : the
      worth
    Of Venice did not fall below her birth,
Venice, the eldest Child of Liberty.
She was a maiden City, bright and free :
    No guile seduced, no force could violate ;
    And when she took unto herself a Mate,
She must espouse the everlasting Sea.
And what if she had seen those glories fade,
    Those titles vanish, and that strength decay ;
Yet shall some tribute of regret be paid
    When her long life hath reached its final
      day ;
Men are we, and must grieve when even the
    Shade
    Of that which once was great is passed away.

WILLIAM WORDSWORTH

To Toussaint L'Ouverture

Toussaint, the most unhappy man of men !
  Whether the whistling Rustic tend his plough
  Within thy hearing, or thy head be now
Pillowed in some deep dungeon's earless den ;—
O miserable Chieftain ! where and when
  Wilt thou find patience ?   Yet die not ; do
    thou
  Wear rather in thy bonds a cheerful brow :
Though fallen thyself, never to rise again,
Live, and take comfort.   Thou hast left behind
  Powers that will work for thee ; air, earth,
    and skies ;
There's not a breathing of the common wind
  That will forget thee ; thou hast great allies;
  Thy friends are exultations, agonies,
And love, and man's unconquerable mind.

WILLIAM WORDSWORTH

INLAND, within a hollow vale, I stood
  And saw, while sea was calm and air was
    clear,
  The coast of France—the coast of France
    how near!
Drawn almost into frightful neighbourhood.
I shrunk; for verily the barrier flood
  Was like a lake, or river bright and fair
  A span of waters; yet what power is there!
What mightiness for evil and for good!
Even so doth God protect us if we be
  Virtuous and wise.   Winds blow, and waters
    roll,
Strength to the brave, and Power, and Deity;
Yet in themselves are nothing!   One decree
  Spake laws to *them*, and said that by the
    soul
Only, the Nations shall be great and free.

WILLIAM WORDSWORTH

WRITTEN IN LONDON. SEPTEMBER 1802

O FRIEND ! I know not which way I must look
  For comfort, being, as I am, opprest,
  To think that now our life is only drest
For show ; mean handiwork of craftsman,
  cook,
Or groom !—We must run glittering like a
  brook
  In the open sunshine, or we are unblest :
  The wealthiest man among us is the best :
No grandeur now in nature or in book
Delights us.   Rapine, avarice, expense,
  This is idolatry ; and these we adore :
  Plain living and high thinking are no more ;
  The homely beauty of the good old cause
Is gone ; our peace, our fearful innocence,
  And pure religion breathing household
  laws.

WILLIAM WORDSWORTH

MILTON ! thou shouldst be living at this hour ;
  England hath need of thee ; she is a fen
  Of stagnant waters ; altar, sword, and pen,
Fireside, the heroic wealth of hall and bower,
Have forfeited their ancient English dower
  Of inward happiness.   We are selfish men ;
  Oh ! raise us up, return to us again ;
And give us manners, virtue, freedom, power.
Thy soul was like a Star, and dwelt apart :
  Thou hadst a voice whose sound was like
    the sea ;
  Pure as the naked heavens, majestic, free,
    So didst thou travel on life's common way,
In cheerful godliness ; and yet thy heart
  The lowliest duties on herself did lay.

WILLIAM WORDSWORTH

GREAT men have been among us ; hands that
    penned
  And tongues that uttered wisdom—better
    none:
The later Sidney, Marvel, Harrington,
Young Vane, and others who called Milton
    friend.
These moralists could act and comprehend :
  They knew how genuine glory was put on ;
  Taught us how rightfully a nation shone
In splendour: what strength was that would
    not bend
But in magnanimous meekness. France, 'tis
    strange,
  Hath brought forth no such souls as we had
    then.
Perpetual emptiness ! unceasing change !
  No single volume paramount, no code,
  No master spirit, no determined road ;
But equally a want of books and men !

WILLIAM WORDSWORTH

IT is not to be thought of that the Flood
   Of British freedom, which, to the open sea
   Of the world's praise, from dark antiquity
Hath flowed, "with pomp of waters, unwith-
     stood,"
Roused though it be full often to a mood
   Which spurns the check of salutary bands,—
   That this most famous Stream in bogs and
     sands
Should perish; and to evil and to good
Be lost for ever.   In our halls is hung
   Armoury of the invincible Knights of old:
We must be free or die, who speak the tongue
   That Shakespeare spake; the faith and
     morals hold
Which Milton held.—In every thing we are
     sprung
   Of Earth's first blood, have titles manifold.

WILLIAM WORDSWORTH

WHEN I have borne in memory what has
    tamed
  Great nations, how ennobling thoughts de-
    part
  When men change swords for ledgers, and
    desert
The student's bower for gold, some fears un-
    named
I had, my country !—am I to be blamed ?
  But when I think of thee, and what thou art,
  Verily, in the bottom of my heart,
Of those unfilial fears I am ashamed.
But dearly must we prize thee ; we who find
  In thee a bulwark for the cause of men ;
    And I by my affection was beguiled.
  What wonder if a poet now and then,
Among the many movements of his mind,
    Felt for thee as a lover or a child ?

WILLIAM WORDSWORTH

Wings have we,—and as far as we can go
    We may find pleasure: wilderness and
      wood,
    Blank ocean and mere sky, support that
      mood
Which with the lofty sanctifies the low.
Dreams, books, are each a world; and books,
    we know,
    Are a substantial world, both pure and
      good:
    Round these, with tendrils strong as flesh
      and blood,
Our pastime and our happiness will grow.
There find I personal themes, a plenteous
    store;
    Matter wherein right voluble I am,
      To which I listen with a ready ear;
      Two shall be named, pre-eminently
        dear,—
The gentle Lady married to the Moor;
    And heavenly Una with her milk-white
      Lamb.

WILLIAM WORDSWORTH

ADMONITION.

WELL mayst thou halt, and gaze with bright-
ening eye !
The lovely cottage in the guardian nook
Hath stirred thee deeply ; with its own dear
brook,
Its own small pasture, almost its own sky !
But covet not the abode ;—forbear to sigh,
As many do, repining while they look ;
Intruders—who would tear from nature's
book
This precious leaf, with harsh impiety.
Think what the home must be if it were thine,
Even thine, though few thy wants !—Roof,
window, door,
The very flowers are sacred to the poor,
The roses to the porch which they entwine :
Yea, all, that now enchants thee, from the
day
On which it should be touched, would melt
away.

THE world is too much with us ; late and
    soon,
  Getting and spending, we lay waste our
    powers :
  Little we see in Nature that is ours ;
We have given our hearts away, a sordid boon !
This Sea that bares her bosom to the moon ;
  The winds that will be howling at all hours,
  And are up-gathered now like sleeping
    flowers ;
For this, for every thing, we are out of tune ;
It moves us not.—Great God ! I'd rather be
  A Pagan suckled in a creed outworn ;
So might I, standing on this pleasant lea,
  Have glimpses that would make me less for-
    lorn ;
Have sight of Proteus rising from the sea ;
  Or hear old Triton blow his wreathèd horn.

WITH ships the sea was sprinkled far and nigh,
 Like stars in heaven, and joyously it
 showed ;
 Some lying fast at anchor in the road,
Some veering up and down, one knew not
 why.
A goodly vessel did I then espy
 Come like a giant from a haven broad ;
 And lustily along the bay she strode,
Her tackling rich, and of apparel high.
This ship was nought to me, nor I to her,
 Yet I pursued her with a lover's look ;
This ship to all the rest did I prefer :
 When will she turn, and whither ? She will
 brook
No tarrying ; where she comes the winds must
 stir :
 On went She,—and due north her journey
 took.

WHERE lies the land to which yon ship must
   go?
  Fresh as a lark mounting at break of day
  Festively she puts forth in trim array ;
Is she for tropic suns, or polar snow?
What boots the inquiry?—Neither friend nor
   foe
  She cares for ; let her travel where she may,
  She finds familiar names, a beaten way
Ever before her, and a wind to blow.
Yet still I ask, what haven is her mark?
  And, almost as it was when ships were rare,
  (From time to time, like pilgrims, here and
   there
Crossing the waters) doubt, and something
   dark,
  Of the old sea some reverential fear,
Is with me at thy farewell, joyous bark !

To Sleep

A FLOCK of sheep that leisurely pass by,
  One after one ; the sound of rain, and bees
  Murmuring ; the fall of rivers, winds, and
    seas,
Smooth fields, white sheets of water, and pure
    sky ;—
I have thought of all by turns, and yet do lie
  Sleepless ; and soon the small birds' melo-
    dies
  Must hear, first uttered from my orchard
    trees ;
And the first cuckoo's melancholy cry.
Even thus last night, and two nights more, I
    lay,
  And could not win thee, Sleep ! by any
    stealth :
So do not let me wear to-night away :
  Without Thee what is all the morning's
    wealth ?
Come, blessèd barrier between day and day,
  Dear mother of fresh thoughts and joyous
    health !

WILLIAM WORDSWORTH

THOUGHT OF A BRITON ON THE SUBJUGATION OF
SWITZERLAND

Two Voices are there ; one is of the Sea,
  One of the Mountains ; each a mighty
    Voice :
  In both from age to age thou didst rejoice,
They were thy chosen music, Liberty !
There came a Tyrant, and with holy glee
  Thou foughtst against him ; but hast vainly
    striven :
  Thou from thy Alpine holds at length art
    driven,
Where not a torrent murmurs heard by thee.
Of one deep bliss thine ear hath been bereft :
Then cleave, O cleave to that which still is
    left ;
  For, high-souled Maid, what sorrow would
    it be
That Mountain floods should thunder as before,
And Ocean bellow from his rocky shore,
  And neither awful Voice be heard by thee !

WILLIAM WORDSWORTH

To B. R. Haydon

HIGH is our calling, Friend !—Creative Art
  (Whether the instrument of words she use,
  Or pencil pregnant with ethereal hues,)
Demands the service of a mind and heart,
Though sensitive, yet, in their weakest part,
  Heroically fashioned—to infuse
  Faith in the whispers of the lonely Muse,
While the whole world seems adverse to desert.
And, oh ! when Nature sinks, as oft she may,
  Through long-lived pressure of obscure dis-
     tress,
    Still to be strenuous for the bright reward,
And in the soul admit of no decay,
  Brook no continuance of weak-mindedness—
  Great is the glory, for the strife is hard !

SURPRISED by joy—impatient as the Wind
  I turned to share the transport—Oh ! with
    whom
  But Thee, deep buried in the silent tomb,
That spot which no vicissitude can find ?
Love, faithful love, recalled thee to my mind—
  But how could I forget thee ?—Through
    what power,
  Even for the least division of an hour,
Have I been so beguiled as to be blind
To my most grievous loss !—That thought's
    return
  Was the worst pang that sorrow ever bore,
Save one, one only, when I stood forlorn,
  Knowing my heart's best treasure was no
    more ;
That neither present time, nor years unborn,
  Could to my sight that heavenly face restore.

WILLIAM WORDSWORTH

THERE is a little unpretending Rill
  Of limpid water, humbler far than aught
  That ever among Men or Naiads sought
Notice or name !—It quivers down the hill
Furrowing its shallow way with dubious will ;
  Yet to my mind this scanty Stream is
    brought
  Oftener than Ganges or the Nile; a thought
Of private recollection sweet and still !
Months perish with their moons ; year treads
    on year ;
  But, faithful Emma, thou with me canst say
That, while ten thousand pleasures disappear,
  And flies their memory fast almost as they,
  The immortal Spirit of one happy day
Lingers beside that Rill, in vision clear.

WILLIAM WORDSWORTH

After-Thought
(River Duddon)

I THOUGHT of Thee, my partner and my guide,
As being past away. — Vain sympathies !
For, backward, Duddon ! as I cast my eyes,
I see what was, and is, and will abide;
Still glides the Stream, and shall for ever glide ;
The Form remains, the Function never dies ;
While we, the brave, the mighty, and the
wise,
We Men, who in our morn of youth defied
The elements, must vanish ;—be it so !
Enough, if something from our hands have
power
To live, and act, and serve the future hour :
And if, as toward the silent tomb we go,
Through love, through hope, and faith's
transcendent dower,
We feel that we are greater than we know.

WILLIAM WORDSWORTH

WALTON'S BOOK OF LIVES

THERE are no colours in the fairest sky
  So fair as these.   The feather whence the
    pen
  Was shaped that traced the lives of these
    good men
Dropped from an angel's wing.   With moist-
    ened eye
We read of faith and purest charity
  In statesman, priest, and humble citizen.
  Oh, could we copy their mild virtues, then
What joy to live, what blessedness to die!
Methinks their very names shine still and
      bright;
Apart, like glow-worms on a summer night;
  Or lonely tapers when from far they fling
A guiding ray; or seen, like stars on high,
  Satellites burning in a lucid ring
Around meek Walton's heavenly memory.

WILLIAM WORDSWORTH

TAX not the royal Saint with vain expense,
  With ill-matched aims the Architect who
    planned—
  Albeit labouring for a scanty band
Of white-robed Scholars only—this immense
And glorious work of fine intelligence !
  Give all thou canst ; high Heaven rejects the
    lore
  Of nicely-calculated less or more ;
So deemed the man who fashioned for the
  sense
These lofty pillars, spread that branching roof
  Self-poised, and scooped into ten thousand
    cells,
  Where light and shade repose, where music
    dwells
    Lingering—and wandering on as loth to
    die ;
Like thoughts whose very sweetness yieldeth
  proof
  That they were born for immortality.

148

MUTABILITY

FROM low to high doth dissolution climb,
  And sink from high to low, along a scale
  Of awful notes, whose concord shall not fail;
A musical but melancholy chime,
Which they can hear who meddle not with
    crime,
  Nor avarice, nor over-anxious care.
  Truth fails not; but her outward forms that
    bear
The longest date do melt like frosty rime,
That in the morning whitened hill and plain
  And is no more; drop like the tower sub-
    lime
  Of yesterday, which royally did wear
Its crown of weeds, but could not even sustain
  Some casual shout that broke the silent
    air,
  Or the unimaginable touch of Time.

WILLIAM WORDSWORTH

THE TROSSACHS

THERE'S not a nook within this solemn Pass,
　But were an apt confessional for One
　Taught by his summer spent, his autumn
　　gone,
That Life is but a tale of morning grass,
Withered at eve.　From scenes of art which
　　chase
　That thought away, turn, and with watchful
　　eyes
　Feed it 'mid Nature's old felicities,
Rocks, rivers, and smooth lakes more clear
　　than glass
Untouched, unbreathed upon.　Thrice happy
　　quest,
　If from a golden perch of aspen spray
　(October's workmanship to rival May)
The pensive warbler of the ruddy breast
　That moral sweeten by a heaven-taught lay,
Lulling the year, with all its cares, to rest.

WILLIAM WORDSWORTH

To the Planet Venus, an Evening Star
COMPOSED AT LOCH LOMOND

Though joy attend thee orient at the birth
  Of dawn, it cheers the lofty spirit most
To watch thy course when Day-light, fled from
    earth,
  In the grey sky hath left his lingering ghost,
Perplexed as if between a splendour lost
  And splendour slowly mustering. Since the
    Sun,
  The absolute, the world-absorbing One,
Relinquished half his empire to the host
Emboldened by thy guidance, holy Star,
  Holy as princely—who that looks on thee
  Touching, as now, in thy humility
The mountain borders of this seat of care,
  Can question that thy countenance is bright,
  Celestial Power, as much with love as light?

WILLIAM WORDSWORTH

A POINT of life between my Parents' dust,
   And yours, my buried Little-ones! am I;
   And to those graves looking habitually
In kindred quiet I repose my trust.
Death to the innocent is more than just,
   And, to the sinner, mercifully bent;
   So may I hope, if truly I repent
And meekly bear the ills which bear I must:
And You, my Offspring! that do still remain,
   Yet may outstrip me in the appointed race,
If e'er, through fault of mine, in mutual pain
   We breathed together for a moment's space,
The wrong, by love provoked, let love arraign,
   And only love keep in your hearts a place.

WILLIAM WORDSWORTH

DEAR to the Loves, and to the Graces vowed,
  The Queen drew back the wimple that she
    wore;
And to the throng how touchingly she bowed
  That hailed her landing on the Cumbrian
    shore;
Bright as a Star (that, from a sombre cloud
  Of pine-tree foliage poised in air, forth darts,
  When a soft summer gale at evening parts
The gloom that did its loveliness enshroud)
She smiled; but Time, the old Saturnian Seer,
  Sighed on the wing as her foot pressed the
    strand,
    With step prelusive to a long array
Of woes and degradations hand in hand,
Weeping captivity, and shuddering fear
    Stilled by the ensanguined block of
    Fotheringay!

MOST sweet it is with unuplifted eyes
    To pace the ground if path there be or none,
While a fair region round the traveller lies,
    Which he forbears again to look upon ;
Pleased rather with some soft ideal scene,
    The work of Fancy or some happy tone
Of meditation, stepping in between
    The beauty coming and the beauty gone.
If Thought and Love desert us, from that day
    Let us break off all commerce with the
        Muse ;
With Thought and Love companions of our
        way,
    Whate'er the senses take or may refuse,
    The Mind's internal heaven shall shed her
        dews
Of inspiration on the humblest lay.

WILLIAM WORDSWORTH

Why art thou silent? Is thy love a plant
  Of such weak fibre that the treacherous air
  Of absence withers what was once so fair?
Is there no debt to pay, no boon to grant?
Yet have my thoughts for thee been vigilant—
  Bound to thy service with unceasing care,
The mind's least generous wish a mendicant
  For naught but what thy happiness could
    spare.
Speak, though this soft warm heart, once free
    to hold
  A thousand tender pleasures, thine and
    mine,
Be left more desolate, more dreary cold
  Than a forsaken bird's-nest filled with
    snow
  'Mid its own bush of leafless eglantine;
  Speak, that my torturing doubts their end
    may know!

WILLIAM WORDSWORTH

COMPOSED ON A MAY MORNING, 1838

LIFE with yon Lambs, like day, is just begun,
   Yet nature seems to them a heavenly guide.
   Does joy approach? they meet the coming
     tide ;
And sullenness avoid, as now they shun
Pale twilight's lingering glooms,—and in the
     sun
   Couch near their dams, with quiet satisfied ;
   Or gambol—each with his shadow at his
     side,
Varying its shape wherever he may run.
As they from turf yet hoar with sleepy dew
   All turn, and court the shining and the
     green,
   Where herbs look up, and opening flowers
     are seen ;
Why to God's goodness cannot We be true,
   And so, His gifts and promises between,
Feed to the last on pleasures ever new ?

WILLIAM WORDSWORTH

THOUGH the bold wings of Poesy affect
    The clouds, and wheel around the mountain
        tops
    Rejoicing, from her loftiest height she drops
Well pleased to skim the plain with wild
        flowers deckt,
Or muse in solemn grove whose shades protect
    The lingering dew—there steals along, or
        stops,
    Watching the least small bird that round
        her hops,
Or creeping worm, with sensitive respect.
Her functions are they therefore less divine,
    Her thoughts less deep, or void of grave
        intent
Her simplest fancies? Should that fear be
        thine,
    Aspiring Votary, ere thy hand present
One offering, kneel before her modest shrine,
    With brow in penitential sorrow bent!
              William Wordsworth.

Samuel Taylor Coleridge

(1772–1834)

To Nature

IT may indeed be phantasy when I
  Essay to draw from all created things
  Deep, heartfelt, inward joy that closely
    clings;
And trace in leaves and flowers that round me
    lie
Lessons of love and earnest piety.
  So let it be; and if the wide world rings
  In mock of this belief, to me it brings
Nor fear, nor grief, nor vain perplexity.
So will I build my altar in the fields,
  And the blue sky my fretted dome shall be,
And the sweet fragrance that the wild flower
    yields,
  Shall be the incense I will yield to Thee,
    Thee only God! and Thou shalt not
      despise
    Even me, the priest of this poor sacrifice.

SAMUEL TAYLOR COLERIDGE

OR THE POET IN THE CLOUDS

O IT is pleasant, with a heart at ease,
    Just after sunset, or by moonlight skies,
To make the shifting clouds be what you
        please,
    Or let the easily-persuaded eyes
Own each quaint likeness issuing from the
        mould
    Of a friend's fancy; or, with head bent
        low
And cheek aslant, see rivers flow of gold
    'Twixt crimson banks; and then, a traveller,
        go
From mount to mount through Cloudland,
        gorgeous land !
    Or listening to the tide, with closèd sight,
Be that blind bard who, on the Chian strand
    By those deep sounds possessed with inward
        light,
      Beheld the Iliad and the Odyssee
      Rise to the swelling of the voiceful sea.

Samuel Taylor Coleridge.

𝔐𝔞𝔯𝔶 𝔗𝔦𝔤𝔟𝔢

To Time

YES, gentle Time, thy gradual, healing hand
   Hath stolen from Sorrow's grasp the en-
      venomed dart;
   Submitting to thy skill, my passive heart
Feels that no grief can thy soft power with-
      stand;
   And though my aching breast still heaves
      the sigh,
   Though oft the tear swells silent in mine
      eye;
Yet the keen pang, the agony is gone;
   Sorrow and I shall part; and these faint
      throes
   Are but the remnant of severer woes:
As when the furious tempest is o'erblown,
   And when the sky has wept its violence,
The opening heavens will oft let fall a shower,
   The poor o'erchargèd boughs still drops
      dispense,
And still the loaded streams in torrents pour.

Charles Lamb

(1775–1834)

O LIFT with reverent hand that tarnished
flower,
That shrines beneath her modest canopy,
Memorials dear to Romish piety,—
Dim specks, rude shapes, of Saints ! in fervent
hour
The work perchance of some weak devotee
Who, poor in worldly treasures to set forth
The sanctities she worshipped to their worth,
In this imperfect tracery might see
Hints, that all Heaven did to her sense reveal.
Cheap gifts best fit poor givers. We are
told
Of the lone mite, the cup of water cold,
That in their way approved the offerer's zeal.
True Love shows costliest where the
means are scant ;
And, in her reckoning, they *abound* who
want.

161

Joseph Blanco White

(1775–1841)

NIGHT AND DEATH

MYSTERIOUS Night! when our first parent knew
  Thee from report divine, and heard thy name,
  Did he not tremble for this lovely frame,
This glorious canopy of light and blue.
Yet 'neath a curtain of translucent dew,
  Bathed in the rays of the great setting flame,
  Hesperus with the host of heaven came,
And lo! creation widened in man's view.
Who could have thought such darkness lay concealed
  Within thy beams, O Sun! or who could find,
Whilst fly and leaf and insect stood revealed,
  That to such countless orbs thou mad'st us blind!
    Why do we then shun Death with anxious strife?
    If Light can thus deceive, wherefore not Life?

William Stanley Roscoe
(1782–1843)

To the Harvest Moon

AGAIN thou reignest in thy golden hall,
  Rejoicing in thy sway, fair queen of night!
  The ruddy reapers hail thee with delight :
Theirs is the harvest, theirs the joyous call
For tasks well ended ere the season's fall.
  Sweet orb, thou smilest from thy starry
    height ;
  But whilst on them thy beams are shedding
    bright
To me thou com'st o'ershadowed with a pall ;
To me alone the year hath fruitless flown ;
  Earth hath fulfilled her trust through all her
    lands,
The good man gathereth where he had sown,
  And the Great Master in his vineyard stands ;
But I, as if my task were all unknown,
  Come to his gates, alas ! with empty hands.

Leigh Hunt

(1784–1859)

To the Grasshopper and the Cricket

GREEN little vaulter in the sunny grass,
  Catching your heart up at the feel of June,
  Sole voice that's heard amidst the lazy noon,
When even the bees lag at the summoning
      brass ;
And you, warm little housekeeper, who class
  With those who think the candles come too
      soon,
  Loving the fire, and with your tricksome
      tune
Nick the glad silent moments as they pass ;
Oh sweet and tiny cousins, that belong,
  One to the fields, the other to the hearth,
Both have your sunshine ; both though small
      are strong
  At your clear hearts ; and both were sent
      on earth
To sing in thoughtful ears this natural song :
  In doors and out, summer and winter,
      Mirth.

164

LEIGH HUNT

The Nile

It flows through all hushed Ægypt and its
    sands,
    Like some grave mighty thought threading
    a dream,
    And times and things, as in that vision,
    seem
Keeping along it their eternal stands,
Caves, pillars, pyramids, the shepherd bands
    That roamed through the young world, the
    glory extreme
    Of high Sesostris, and that southern beam,
The laughing queen that caught the world's
    great hands.
Then comes a mightier silence, stern and
    strong,
As of a world left empty of its throng,
    And the void weighs on us ; and then we
    wake,
And hear the fruitful stream lapsing along
    'Twixt villages, and think how we shall take
    Our own calm journey on for human sake.
                  Leigh Hunt.

George Gordon, Lord Byron

(1788–1859)

ON CHILLON

ETERNAL Spirit of the chainless Mind!
  Brightest in dungeons, Liberty, thou art—
  For there thy habitation is the heart—
The heart which love of thee alone can
    bind;
And when thy sons to fetters are consigned,
  To fetters, and the damp vault's dayless
    gloom,
  Their country conquers with their martyr-
    dom,
And Freedom's fame finds wings on every
    wind.
Chillon! thy prison is a holy place,
  And thy sad floor an altar, for 'twas trod,
Until his very steps have left a trace
  Worn as if thy cold pavement were a sod,
By Bonnivard! May none those marks efface!
  For they appeal from tyranny to God.

166

Sir Aubrey de Vere

(1788–1846)

THE CHILDREN BAND
THE CRUSADERS. NO. V.

ALL holy influences dwell within
   The breast of Childhood : instincts fresh
     from God
   Inspire it, ere the heart beneath the rod
Of grief hath bled, or caught the plague of sin.
How mighty was that fervour which could
     win
   Its way to infant souls !—and was the sod
   Of Palestine by infant Croises trod ?
Like Joseph went they forth, or Benjamin,
In all their touching beauty, to redeem?
   And did their soft lips kiss the sepulchre ?
Alas ! the lovely pageant, as a dream,
   Faded ! they sank not through ignoble fear;
They felt not Moslem steel. By mountain,
     stream,
   In sands, in fens, they died—no mother
     near !

Bryan Waller Procter

(1790–1874)

A Still Place

UNDER what beechen shade or silent oak
　Lies the mute sylvan now mysterious Pan?
　Once (when rich Péneus and Ilissus ran
Clear from their fountains) as the morning
　　broke,
'Tis said the Satyr with Apollo spoke,
　And to harmonious strife with his wild reed,
　Challenged the God, whose music was in-
　　deed
Divine, and fit for heaven. Each played,
　　and woke
Beautiful sounds to life—deep melodies ;
　One blew his pastoral pipe with such nice
　　care,
That flocks and birds all answered him ; and
　　one
　Shook his immortal showers upon the air.
That music has ascended to the sun;
But where the other? Speak, ye dells and
　　trees.

BRYAN WALLER PROCTER

The Sea—In Calm

Look what immortal floods the sunset pours
    Upon us!—Mark how still (as though in
      dreams
    Bound) the once wild and terrible Ocean
      seems!
How silent are the winds!   No billow roars,
But all is tranquil as Elysian shores;
    The silver margin which aye runneth round
    The moon-enchanted sea hath here no sound:
Even Echo speaks not on these radiant moors.
What! is the giant of the ocean dead,
    Whose strength was all unmatched beneath
      the sun?
    No: he reposes.   Now his toils are done,
    More quiet than the babbling brooks is he.
So mightiest powers by deepest calms are fed,
    And sleep, how oft, in things that gent-
      lest be.

Bryan Waller Procter.

Percy Bysshe Shelley

(1790–1882)

OZYMANDIAS

I MET a traveller from an antique land
  Who said : Two vast and trunkless legs of
    stone
Stand in the desert.   Near them, on the sand,
  Half sunk, a shattered visage lies, whose
    frown
And wrinkled lip and sneer of cold command
  Tell that its sculptor well those passions read
Which yet survive, stamped on these lifeless
    things,
    The hand that mocked them and the heart
      that fed ;
    And on the pedestal these words appear :
" My name is Ozymandias, king of kings :
  Look on my works, ye Mighty, and
    despair ! "
Nothing beside remains.   Round the decay
  Of that colossal wreck, boundless and bare
The lone and level sands stretch far away.

John Keble
(1792–1866)

At Hooker's Tomb

THE grey-eyed Morn was saddened with a
    shower,
  A silent shower, that trickled down so still
Scarce dropped beneath its weight the ten-
    derest flower,
    Scarce could you trace it on the twinkling rill,
Or moss-stone bathed in dew. It was an
    hour
    Most meet for prayer beside thy lowly
    grave,
Most for thanksgiving meet, that Heaven
    such power
    To thy serene and humble spirit gave.
"Who sow good seed with tears shall reap
    in joy."
    So thought I as I watched the gracious
    rain,
And deemed it like that silent sad employ
    Whence sprung thy glory's harvest, to re-
    main
    For ever. God hath sworn to lift on
    high
    Who sinks himself by true humility.

Felicia Dorothea Hemans

(1794–1835)

FLIGHT OF THE SPIRIT

WHITHER, oh! whither wilt thou wing thy
    way?
What solemn region first upon thy sight
Shall break, unveiled for terror or delight?
What hosts, magnificent in dread array,
My spirit! when thy prison-house of clay
    After long strife is rent?   Fond, fruitless
    quest!
The unfledged bird, within his narrow nest,
Sees but a few green branches o'er him play,
And through their parting leaves, by fits
    revealed,
A glimpse of summer sky; nor knows the
    field
    Wherein his dormant powers must yet be
    tried.
        Thou art that bird!—of what beyond thee
        lies
        Far in the untracked, immeasurable skies
Knowing but this—that thou shalt find thy
    Guide!

John Keats

(1793–1821)

ON FIRST LOOKING INTO CHAPMAN'S HOMER.

MUCH have I travelled in the realms of gold
    And many goodly states and kingdoms seen ;
    Round many western islands have I been
Which bards in fealty to Apollo hold.
Oft of one wide expanse had I been told
    That deep-browed Homer ruled as his de-
        mesne ;
    Yet did I never breathe its pure serene
Till I heard Chapman speak out loud and
        bold :
Then felt I like some watcher of the skies
    When a new planet swims into his ken ;
Or like stout Cortez, when with eagle eyes
    He stared at the Pacific—and all his men
Looked at each other with a wild surmise—
    Silent, upon a peak in Darien.

JOHN KEATS

ON THE GRASSHOPPER AND CRICKET

THE poetry of earth is never dead :
  When all the birds are faint with the hot
    sun,
  And hide in cooling trees, a voice will run
From hedge to hedge about the new-mown
    mead ;
That is the Grasshopper's—he takes the lead
  In summer luxury—he has never done
  With his delights ; for when tired out with
    fun,
He rests at ease beneath some pleasant weed.
The poetry of earth is ceasing never :
  On a lone winter evening, when the frost
    Has wrought a silence, from the stove
    there shrills
The Cricket's song, in warmth increasing ever,
  And seems to one in drowsiness half lost,
    The Grasshopper's among some grassy
    hills.

JOHN KEATS

To one who has been long in city pent,
   'Tis very sweet to look into the fair
   And open face of heaven—to breathe a
     prayer
Full in the smile of the blue firmament.
Who is more happy, when, with heart's con-
     tent,
   Fatigued he sinks into some pleasant lair
   Of wavy grass, and reads a debonair
And gentle tale of love and languishment?
Returning home at evening, with an ear
   Catching the notes of Philomel—an eye
Watching the sailing cloudlet's bright career,
   He mourns that day so soon has glided by;
E'en like the passage of an angel's tear
   That falls through the clear ether silently.

JOHN KEATS

AFTER dark vapours have oppressed our plains
  For a long dreary season, comes a day
  Born of the gentle South, and clears away
From the sick heavens all unseemly stains.
The anxious month, relievèd from its pains,
  Takes as a long-lost right the feel of May,
  The eyelids with the passing coolness play,
Like rose-leaves with the drip of summer rains.
The calmest thoughts come round us—as, of
    leaves
  Budding—fruit ripening in stillness—autumn
    suns
Smiling at eve upon the quiet sheaves,—
Sweet Sappho's cheek,—a sleeping infant's
    breath,—
  The gradual sand that through an hour-glass
    runs,—
A woodland rivulet,—a Poet's death.

JOHN KEATS

ON A PICTURE OF LEANDER

COME hither, all sweet maidens soberly,
   Down-looking aye, and with a chasten'd
     light,
   Hid in the fringes of your eyelids white,
And meekly let your fair hands joinèd be,
As if so gentle that ye could not see,
   Untouch'd, a victim of your beauty bright,
   Sinking away to his young spirit's night,
Sinking bewilder'd 'mid the dreary sea :
'Tis young Leander toiling to his death ;
   Nigh swooning, he doth purse his weary
     lips
For Hero's cheek, and smiles against her smile.
   O horrid dream ! see how his body dips
Dead-heavy ; arms and shoulders gleam awhile ;
He's gone ; up bubbles all his amorous breath !

JOHN KEATS

When I have fears that I may cease to be
    Before my pen has gleaned my teeming
      brain,
Before high-pilèd books, in charact'ry,
    Hold like full garners the full-ripened grain;
When I behold, upon the night's starred face,
    Huge cloudy symbols of a high romance,
And feel that I may never live to trace
    Their shadows, with the magic hand of
      chance;
And when I feel, fair creature of an hour!
    That I shall never look upon thee more,
Never have relish in the faery power
    Of unreflecting love! then on the shore
Of the wide world I stand alone, and think,
Till Love and Fame to nothingness do sink.

JOHN KEATS

IF by dull rhymes our English must be chained,
    And, like Andromeda, the Sonnet sweet
Fettered, in spite of painèd loveliness ;
Let us find out if we must be constrained,
    Sandals more interwoven and complete
To fit the naked foot of poesy ;
Let us inspect the lyre, and weigh the stress
Of every chord, and see what may be gained
    By ear industrious, and attention meet ;
Misers of sound and syllable, no less
Than Midas of his coinage, let us be
    Jealous of dead leaves in that bay wreath
      crown ;
So, if we may not let the Muse be free,
    She will be bound with garlands of her own.

JOHN KEATS

To Sleep

O SOFT embalmer of the still midnight !
  Shutting with careful fingers and benign,
Our gloom-pleased eyes, embowered from the
    light,
  Enshaded in forgetfulness divine ;
O soothest Sleep ! if so it please thee, close,
  In midst of this thine hymn, my willing
    eyes,
Or wait the amen, ere thy poppy throws
  Around my bed its lulling charities ;
  Then save me, or the passèd day will shine
Upon my pillow, breeding many woes ;
  Save me from curious conscience, that still
    lords
Its strength, for darkness burrowing like a
    mole ;
  Turn the key deftly in the oiled wards,
And seal the hushèd casket of my soul.

JOHN KEATS

Bright *STAR!* would I were steadfast as thou
    art—
  Not in lone splendour hung aloft the night,
And watching with eternal lids apart,
  Like Nature's patient, sleepless Eremite,
The moving waters at their priest-like task
  Of pure ablution round earth's human shores,
Or gazing on the new soft fallen mask
  Of snow upon the mountains and the moors—
No—yet still steadfast, still unchangeable,
  Pillowed upon my fair love's ripening breast,
To feel for ever its soft fall and swell,
  Awake for ever in a sweet unrest,
Still, still to hear her tender-taken breath,
And so live ever—or else swoon to death.

John Keats.

Ibartley Coleridge

(1796–1849)

To Night

THE crackling embers on the hearth are dead ;
  The indoor note of industry is still ;
  The latch is fast ; upon the window-sill
The small birds wait not for their daily bread ;
The voiceless flowers—how quietly they shed
    Their nightly odours ; and the household
      ill
  Murmurs continuous dulcet sounds that fill
The vacant expectation, and the dread
Of listening night. And haply now She
    sleeps ;
  For all the garrulous noises of the air
Are hushed in peace ; the soft dew silent
    weeps,
  Like hopeless lovers for a maid so fair :—
Oh ! that I were the happy dream that creeps
  To her soft heart, to find my image there.

To Shakspeare

The soul of man is larger than the sky,
   Deeper than ocean, or the abysmal dark
   Of the unfathomed centre.   Like that Ark,
Which in its sacred hold uplifted high,
O'er the drowned hills, the human family,
   And stock reserved of every living kind ;
   So, in the compass of the single mind,
The seeds and pregnant forms in essence lie
That make all worlds.   Great poet, 'twas thy
     art
   To know thyself, and in thyself to be
   Whate'er love, hate, ambition, destiny,
Or the firm, fatal purpose of the heart,
     Can make of Man.   Yet thou wert still
      the same,
     Serene of thought, unhurt by thy own
      flame.

Not in Vain

Let me not deem that I was made in vain,
  Or that my being was an accident
  Which Fate, in working its sublime intent,
Not wished to be, to hinder would not deign.
Each drop uncounted in a storm of rain
  Hath its own mission, and is duly sent
  To its own leaf or blade, not idly spent
'Mid myriad dimples on the shipless main.
The very shadow of an insect's wing,
  For which the violet cared not while it
    stayed
Yet felt the lighter for its vanishing,
  Proved that the sun was shining by its shade
Then can a drop of the eternal spring,
  Shadow of living lights, in vain be made?

PRAYER I

THERE is an awful quiet in the air,
  And the sad earth, with moist imploring
    eye,
  Looks wide and wakeful at the pondering
    sky,
Like Patience slow-subsiding to Despair.
But see, the blue smoke as a voiceless prayer,
  Sole witness of a secret sacrifice,
  Unfolds its tardy wreaths, and multiplies
Its soft chameleon breathings in the rare
Capacious ether,—so it fades away,
  And nought is seen beneath the pendent
    blue,
The undistinguishable waste of day.
  So have I dreamed !—oh, may the dream be
    true !—
  That praying souls are purged from mortal
    hue,
And grow as pure as He to whom they pray.

PRAYER II

BE not afraid to pray—to pray is right.
    Pray, if thou canst, with hope; but ever
        pray,
    Though hope be weak, or sick with long
        delay;
Pray in the darkness, if there be no light.
Far is the time, remote from human sight,
    When war and discord on the earth shall
        cease;
    Yet every prayer for universal peace
Avails the blessèd time to expedite.
Whate'er is good to wish, ask that of Heaven,
    Though it be what thou canst not hope to
        see:
Pray to be perfect, though material leaven
    Forbid the spirit so on earth to be;
But if for any wish thou darest not pray,
Then pray to God to cast that wish away.

Hartley Coleridge.

Thomas Hood

(1798–1845)

SILENCE

THERE is a silence where hath been no sound;
  There is a silence where no sound may be
  In the cold grave—under the deep, deep sea,
Or in wide desert where no life is found,
Which hath been mute, and still must sleep
    profound ;
  No voice is hushed—no life treads silently,
  But clouds and cloudy shadows wander free
That never spoke, over the idle ground.
But in green ruins, in the desolate walls
  Of antique palaces, where Man hath been,
Though the dun fox, or wild hyæna, calls,
  And owls, that flit continually between,
Shriek to the echo, and the low winds moan,
There the true Silence is, self-conscious and
    alone.

THOMAS HOOD

DEATH

IT is not death, that sometime in a sigh
  This eloquent breath shall take its speechless
    flight;
That sometime these bright stars, that now
    reply
  In sunlight to the sun, shall set in night,
  That this warm conscious flesh shall perish
    quite,
And all life's ruddy springs forget to flow;
  That thoughts shall cease, and the immortal
    sprite
Be lapped in alien clay and laid below;
It is not death to know this,—but to know
  That pious thoughts, which visit at new
    graves
In tender pilgrimage, will cease to go
  So duly and so oft,—and when grass waves
Over the past-away, there may be then
No resurrection in the minds of men.

                              Thomas Hood.

Chauncey Hare Townshend
(1800–1868)

GIVE me thy joy in sorrow, gracious Lord,
   And sorrow's self shall like to joy appear !
   Although the world should waver in its
     sphere
I tremble not if Thou thy peace afford ;
But, Thou withdrawn, I am but as a chord
   That vibrates to the pulse of hope and
     fear :
   Nor rest I more than harps which to the
     air
Must answer when we place their tuneful
     board
Against the blast, which thrill unmeaning
     woe
   Even in their sweetness. So no earthly
     wing
E'er sweeps me but to sadden. Oh, place
     Thou
   My heart beyond the world's sad vibrating—
     And where but in Thyself? Oh, circle
     me,
     That I may feel no touches save of Thee.

Samuel Laman Blanchard

(1804–1845)

HIDDEN JOYS

PLEASURES lie thickest where no pleasures
  seem :
  There's not a leaf that falls upon the ground
  But holds some joy, of silence or of sound,
Some sprite begotten of a summer dream.
The very meanest things are made supreme
  With innate ecstasy.   No grain of sand
  But moves a bright and million-peopled
  land,
And hath its Edens and its Eves, I deem.
For Love, though blind himself, a curious
  eye
  Hath lent me, to behold the hearts of
  things,
And touched mine ear with power.   Thus, far
  or nigh,
  Minute or mighty, fixed or free with wings,
Delight from many a nameless covert sly
  Peeps sparkling, and in tones familiar sings.

SAMUEL LAMAN BLANCHARD

WISHES OF YOUTH

GAILY and greenly let my seasons run :
  And should the war-winds of the world up-
    root
  The sanctities of life, and its sweet fruit
Cast forth as fuel for the fiery sun;
The dews be turned to ice—fair days begun
  In peace wear out in pain, and sounds that
    suit
  Despair and discord keep Hope's harpstring
    mute;
Still let me live as Love and Life were one :
Still let me turn on earth a child-like gaze,
  And trust the whispered charities that bring
Tidings of human truth ; with inward praise
  Watch the weak motion of each common
    thing
And find it glorious—still let me raise
  On wintry wrecks an altar to the Spring.
                    Samuel Laman Blanchard.

Sir William Rowan Hamilton
(1805–1865)

SPIRIT OF WISDOM AND OF LOVE

O BROODING Spirit of Wisdom and of Love,
  Whose mighty wings even now o'ershadow
    me ;
  Absorb me in thine own immensity,
And raise me far my finite self above !
Purge vanity away and the weak care
  That name or fame of me should widely
    spread ;
  And the deep wish keep burning in their
    stead
Thy blissful influence afar to bear,
Or see it borne ! Let no desire of ease,
  No lack of courage, faith, or love, delay
  My own steps in that high thought-paven
    way,
In which my soul her clear commission sees :
  Yet with an equal joy let me behold
  Thy chariot o'er that way by others roll'd.

192

Elizabeth Barrett Browning
(1809–1861)

CONSOLATION

ALL are not taken ; there are left behind
  Living Beloveds, tender looks to bring
  And make the daylight still a happy thing,
And tender voices, to make soft the wind :
But if it were not so—if I could find
  No love in all the world for comforting,
  Nor any path but hollowly did ring,
Where "dust to dust" the love from life dis-
    joined,
And if, before those sepulchres unmoving
  I stood alone, (as some forsaken lamb
    Goes bleating up the moors in weary
    dearth)
Crying "Where are ye, O my loved and
    loving?"—
  I know a Voice would sound, "Daughter,
    I AM.
    Can I suffice for HEAVEN and not for
    earth?"

193

E. BARRETT BROWNING

GRIEF

I TELL you, hopeless grief is passionless;
   That only men incredulous of despair,
   Half-taught in anguish, through the mid-
      night air
Beat upward to God's throne in loud access
Of shrieking and reproach.   Full desertness
   In souls as countries, lieth silent-bare
   Under the blanching, vertical eye-glare
Of the absolute Heavens. Deep-hearted man,
    express
Grief for thy Dead in silence like to death—
   Most like a monumental statue set
    In everlasting watch and moveless woe,
Till itself crumble to the dust beneath.
   Touch it; the marble eyelids are not wet:
    If it could weep, it would arise and go.

E. BARRETT BROWNING

CHEERFULNESS TAUGHT BY REASON

I THINK we are too ready with complaint
   In this fair world of God's.   Had we no
     hope
   Indeed beyond the zenith and the slope
Of yon grey blank of sky, we might grow
     faint
To muse upon eternity's constraint
   Round our aspirant souls; but since the
     scope
   Must widen early, is it well to droop,
For a few days consumed in loss and taint?
O pusillanimous heart, be comforted
   And, like a cheerful traveller, take the road,
Singing beside the hedge.   What if the bread
   Be bitter in thine inn, and thou unshod
To meet the flints?   At least it may be said,
   Because the way is *short*, I thank thee,
     God.

E. BARRETT BROWNING

But only three in all God's universe
    Have heard this word thou hast said ; Him-
        self, beside
    Thee speaking and me listening ! and re-
        plied
One of us . . . *that* was God ! . . . and laid
        the curse
So darkly on my eyelids as to amerce
    My sight from seeing thee—that if I had
        died,
    The deathweights, placed there, would have
        signified
Less absolute exclusion.   "Nay" is worse
From God than from all others, O my
        friend !
    Men could not part us with their worldly
        jars,
Nor the seas change us, nor the tempests
        bend ;
    Our hands would touch, for all the mountain-
        bars ;—
And, heaven being rolled between us at the
        end
    We should but vow the faster for the stars.

E. BARRETT BROWNING

UNLIKE are we, unlike, O princely Heart!
  Unlike our uses, and our destinies.
  Our ministering two angels look surprise
On one another, as they strike athwart
Their wings in passing. Thou, bethink thee,
    art
  A guest for queens to social pageantries
  With gages from a hundred brighter eyes
Than tears, even, can make mine, to ply thy
    part
Of chief musician. What hast *thou* to do
  With looking from the lattice-lights at me,
A poor, tired, wandering singer? . . . singing
    through
  The dark, and leaning up a cypress tree?
The chrism is on thine head,—on mine, the
    dew —
  And Death must dig the level where these
    agree.

E. BARRETT BROWNING

I LIFT my heavy heart up solemnly,
   As once Electra her sepulchral urn,
   And, looking in thine eyes, I overturn
The ashes at thy feet.   Behold and see
What a great heap of grief lay hid in me,
   And how the red wild sparkles dimly burn
   Through the ashen greyness.   If thy foot in
      scorn
Could tread them out to darkness utterly,
It might be well, perhaps.   But if, instead,
   Thou wait beside me for the wind to blow
The grey dust up, . . . those laurels on thine
      head,
   O my beloved, will not shield thee so,
That none of all the fires shall scorch and
      shred
   The hair beneath.   Stand farther off, then!
   Go.

Go from me.   Yet I feel that I shall stand
   Henceforward in thy shadow.   Nevermore
   Alone upon the threshold of my door
Of individual life, shall I command
The uses of my soul, nor lift my hand
   Serenely in the sunshine as before,
   Without the sense of that which I fore-
     bore . . .
Thy touch upon the palm.   The widest land
Doom takes to part us, leaves thy heart in
     mine
   With pulses that beat double.   What I do
And what I dream include thee, as the wine
   Must taste of its own grapes.   And when I
     sue
God for myself, He hears that name of
     thine,
   And sees within my eyes, the tears of two.

E. BARRETT BROWNING

WHAT can I give thee back, O liberal
  And princely giver, . . . who hast brought
    the gold
  And purple of thine heart, unstained un-
    told,
And laid them on the outside of the wall,
For such as I to take, or leave withal,
  In unexpected largesse?   Am I cold,
  Ungrateful, that for these most manifold
High gifts, I render nothing back at all?
Not so.   Not cold!—but very poor instead!
  Ask God who knows! for frequent tears
    have run
The colours from my life, and left so dead
  And pale a stuff, it were not fitly done
To give the same as pillow to thy head.
  Go farther! Let it serve to trample on.

E. BARRETT BROWNING

IF thou must love me, let it be for nought
  Except for love's sake only.   Do not say,
  "I love her for her smile . . . her look . . .
  her way
Of speaking gently, . . . for a   trick of
  thought
That falls in well with mine, and certes
  brought
  A sense of pleasant ease on such a day"—
  For these things in themselves, Beloved,
  may
Be changed, or change for thee,—and love so
  wrought,
May be unwrought so.   Neither love me for
  Thine own dear pity's wiping my cheeks
  dry,
Since one might well forget to weep who bore
  Thy comfort long, and lose thy love there-
  by,
But love me for love's sake, that evermore
  Thou mayst love on through love's eternity.

E. BARRETT BROWNING

WHEN our two souls stand up erect and
    strong,
  Face to face, silent, drawing nigh and
    nigher,
  Until the lengthening wings break into fire
At either curvèd point,—what bitter wrong
Can the earth do us, that we should not long
  Be here contented?   Think.   In mounting
    higher
  The angels would press on us, and aspire
To drop some golden orb of perfect song
Into our deep, dear silence.   Let us stay
  Rather on earth, Beloved,—where the unfit
Contrarious moods of men recoil away
  And isolate pure spirits, and permit
A place to stand and love in for a day,
  With darkness and the death-hour rounding
    it.

E. BARRETT BROWNING

How do I love thee? Let me count the
 ways.
 I love thee to the depth and breadth and
  height
 My soul can reach, when feeling out of
  sight
For the ends of Being and Ideal Grace.
I love thee to the level of every day's
 Most quiet need, by sun and candlelight.
 I love thee freely, as men strive for Right ;
I love thee purely, as they turn from Praise ;
I love thee with the passion put to use
 In my old griefs, and with my childhood's
  faith ;
I love thee with a love I seemed to lose
 With my lost saints—I love thee, with the
  breath,
Smiles, tears, of all my life !—and, if God
 choose,
 I shall but love thee better after death.
     Elizabeth Barrett Browning.

SCORN not the Sonnet; Critic, you have
    frowned,
    Mindless of its just honours : with this key
    Shakspeare unlocked his heart ; the melody
Of this small lute gave ease to Petrarch's
    wound ;
A thousand times this pipe did Tasso sound ;
    With it Camöens soothed an exile's grief ;
    The Sonnet glittered a gay myrtle leaf
Amid the cypress with which Dante crowned
His visionary brow ; a glow-worm lamp
    It cheered mild Spenser, called from Faery-
    land
To struggle through dark ways ; and when a
    damp
    Fell round the path of Milton, in his hand
    The Thing became a trumpet, whence he
    blew
    Soul-animating strains—alas, too few !
                                    WORDSWORTH.

NOTES

P. 4.—" Prometheus, when first from heaven high."
—In line 3 the printed copies (including that in
England's Helicon, 1600) give "fond of delight."
"Fond of the light" is Dr. Hannah's correction,
from the Harleian MS. For the fancy of this
sonnet, cf. Herrick, *Hesperides*, 565 :

> " I played with Love, as with the fire
> The wanton Satyr did ;
> Nor did I know, or could descry
> What under these was hid.
> That Satyr he but burnt his lips ;
> But mine's the greater smart,
> For kissing Love's dissembling chips
> The fire scorched my heart."

P. 6.—" Happy ye leaves whenas those lily hands."
—The lady of the sonnet—the Elizabeth whom
Spenser married in Ireland on St. Barnabas' Day,
1594, and for whom he wrote his magnificent
Epithalamion—was almost certainly Elizabeth
Boyle, of Kilcoran by the Bay of Youghal, a
kinswoman of the great Earl of Cork. Dr. Grosart
(*Complete Works in Verse and Prose of Edmund
Spenser*, vol. i.) has discovered a grant, made in
1606 by Sir Richard Boyle to Elizabeth Boyle, *alias*
Seckerstone, widow, of her house at Kilcoran for

NOTES

half-a-crown a year. Now it is known that Spenser's widow married our Roger Seckerstone in 1603 ; and it is, to say the least, unlikely that there were two Elizabeth Seckerstones (unusual name !) in the neighbourhood at one time.

"Of Helicon, whence she derivèd is"—cf. Sonnet 11, line 10 : "My *Helice*, the lodestar of my life." *Helice*, it is suggested, stands for Elisé, Elizabeth.

P. 16.—"One day I wrote her name upon the strand." See note preceding. The strand of Kilcoran— three miles long—is famous.

P. 19.—"With how sad steps, O moon, thou climb'st the skies !" "The last line of this poem," says Charles Lamb, "is a little obscured by transposition. He means, 'Do they call ungratefulness there a virtue ? ' "

P. 50.—"Full many a glorious morning have I seen." I suppose that in the last line ("Suns of the world may stain when heaven's sun staineth") "stain" = "be stained"—*i. e.* with clouds. But the context seems to suggest that "stain" may stand for "'stain," "abstain."

P. 95.—"Captain, or Colonel, or Knight in Arms." The date "when the assault was intended" —or at least expected—"to the city" was Nov. 13, 1642. After Edgehill (Oct. 23) the Royal army advanced up the Thames valley upon London ; took Brentford on Nov. 12 ; and on the following day advanced as far as Turnham Green, and were met by the Parliamentarians, 24,000 strong. The two armies "stood many hours in battalia facing one another." It seems to have been a case of "one was afraid and t'other didn't dare." In the end the Royal army, which was short of ammunition, withdrew to Colnbrook.

"The great Emathian conqueror"—Alexander the Great, who was said (see Mr. Mark Pattison's note for authorities) to have spared Pindar's house at the sack of Thebes, B.C. 333. Emathian = Macedonian.

NOTES

"Sad Electra's poet"—Euripides. Milton's authority here is Plutarch, who tells that when the Lacedæmonians took Athens in 404 B.C. they were incited by the Thebans to raze the city to the ground. The decision was in suspense when, as the generals sat at wine together, a Phocian sang part of the chorus from the *Electra*, which so affected all present that they agreed at once it would be an unworthy act to destroy a city that had given birth to such poetry.

P. 97.—"Daughter to that good Earl, once President." The Lady Margaret Ley was daughter of James Ley (1552—1629), made Lord High Treasurer in 1622, Lord President of the Council in 1628, and in that same year advanced to the earldom of Scarborough. His death coincided with the sudden breaking up of the third Parliament of Charles I., and is compared by Milton with the death of the Athenian orator, Isocrates ("that old man eloquent"), after the battle of Chæronea, B.C. 338, when Philip of Macedon destroyed the combined forces of Athens and Thebes. Isocrates (he was in his 99th year, by the way) died four days after receiving the news of Chæronea, just as Ley died four days after the dissolution of Parliament on March 10, 1629.

P. 98.—"Harry, whose tuneful and well-measured song." Henry Lawes, of the Chapel Royal, was Milton's friend from boyhood. He dedicated his book, *Choice Psalmes*, in 1648, to King Charles, then a captive. "It was this Royalist and Cavalier volume to which Milton supplied the recommendatory sonnet. Violent partisan as Milton was he did not allow political feeling to sever the tie of early friendship, or of a common love of musical art."—*Pattison*. Line 4—"committing short and long." Lat. *committere*, to pair, to set together.

P. 100.—"Cromwell, our chief of men, who through a cloud." Not a general testimony to Cromwell's character, but addressed to him on a

207

special emergency. "The moment was one when the question of a ' maintenance for a godly ministry ' was the uppermost question. The Presbyterian party, especially in London and Lancashire, wanted a state-supported church and tithes, or a provision in lieu of tithes, while the Independent party regarded with aversion any interference of the secular arm with spiritual things. The extreme view, shared by Milton, went so far as to look upon payment for spiritual ministration as contrary to the gospel."—*Pattison.*

The "Committee for the Propagation of the Gospel" was a committee of the Rump Parliament, fourteen in number, having general supervision of church affairs, and, in particular, the duty of providing spiritual food for destitute parishes. To this committee "certain ministers," headed by John Owen, had offered fifteen Proposals, in which they asked that preachers should receive a public maintenance.

Line 14.—"Whose gospel is their maw"—cf. *Lycidas* (written in 1637)—

" How well could I have spared for thee, young
    swain,
Enow of such as for their bellies' sake,
Creep, and intrude, and climb into the fold !
Of other care they little reckoning make,
Than how to scramble at the shearers' feast,
And shove away the worthy bidden guest.
Blind mouths ! . . . . "

P. 101.—"Vane, young in years, but in sage counsel old." Sir Henry Vane, the younger, born in 1612, and therefore forty years old at the date of this sonnet, was son of Sir Henry Vane, of Raby Castle, county Durham. He was governor of Massachusetts in 1636, but soon returned to England, entered Parliament, and was appointed Treasurer of the Navy. He took an active part against Strafford, and was principal mover of the

NOTES

Covenant in England and the Self-Denying Ordinance. Although not a regicide, he suffered death on that ground in 1662.

Line 4.—"The fierce Epirot" is Pyrrhus, repelled B.C. 279; and "The African bold," Hannibal. Pattison quotes Duruy, *Histoire des Romaines*, as saying of Hannibal in B.C. 203, "il se sentait vaincu par quelque chose de plus fort que son génie, les mœurs et les institutions de Rome."

P. 102.—"Avenge, O Lord, thy slaughtered saints, whose bones." In Jan. 1655, the Duke of Savoy determined to make the poor Vaudois inhabitants of certain Piedmontese valleys renounce the simple forms of faith and worship they had inherited from days long before Luther, and conform to the Catholic religion. They remonstrated; and in April 1655, a crowd of hired soldiery poured into the valleys and revelled there for many days in rape, pillage, and savage massacre. The news took nearly a month to reach England; but when it came "a cry of horror went through the country . . . . A day of humiliation was appointed, large collections were made for the sufferers, and a special envoy was despatched to remonstrate with the Duke of Savoy." The government despatches in this business were written by Milton.

Lines 7, 8.—"that rolled Mother with infant down the rocks"—"A mother was hurled down a mighty rock with a little infant in her arms; and three days after was found dead with the child alive, but fast claspt between the arms of the mother, which were cold and stiff, insomuch that those that found them had much ado to get the child out."—*Account of the massacre by Sir William Moreland, Cromwell's Agent in Piedmont: published in 1658.*

P. 104. — "Lawrence, of virtuous father virtuous son"—cf. Horace, *Carm.*, line 16, "O matre pulchra filia pulchrior." The Lawrence addressed

209

NOTES

was one of the sons of Henry Lawrence, President of the Council in 1654.

P. 105.—"Cyriack, whose grandsire on the royal bench." The mother of Cyriack Skinner was Bridget, a daughter of the famous Sir Edward Coke.

P. 106.—"Cyriack, this three years' day these eyes, though clear." The allusion in lines 10--12 is to the *Defensio pro populo Anglicano contra Salmasium*, which Milton had persisted in writing, though warned by the physician of the probable consequences to his eyesight.

P. 107.—"Methought I saw my late espousèd saint." Milton on Nov. 12, 1656, married Catherine Woodcock, daughter of Captain Woodcock, of Hackney. After fifteen months of married happiness, she died in child-bed, February 1658, her baby surviving but a month.

P. 108.—"Cambridge, with whom, my pilot and my guide"—Richard Owen Cambridge (1717—1802), now chiefly memorable as the author of *The Scribleriad* (1751).

Line 2.—"Pleased I have traversed thy Sabrina's flood." Cambridge resided at Whitminster in Gloucestershire, close to the Severn, and on the banks of the Stroud which runs into that river. Cf. Chalmers' Memoir : "While he continued to cultivate polite literature, his more active hours were employed in heightening the beauties of the scenery around his seat ; for this purpose he made the little river Stroud navigable for some distance, and not only constructed boats for pleasure or carriage, but introduced some ingenious improvements in that branch of naval architecture, which were approved by the most competent judges."—*Chalmers' English Poets*, vol. 18, p. 227.

Pp. 122-3.—"It was the candle of Bowles that lit the fire of Coleridge," says Mr. Austin Dobson. In a copy of the *Sonnets* (first published in 1789) preserved at South Kensington, Coleridge writes

NOTES

of them as "having done his heart more good than all the other books he ever read excepting his Bible." They have now an historical rather than an intrinsic interest.

P. 129. — "Toussaint, the most unhappy man of men!" François Dominique Toussaint L'Ouverture, son of African slaves, was born in San Domingo, 1743; appointed chief of the army of San Domingo by the Directory in 1796, and ruled the island with justice and vigour. In 1801, when Bonaparte sought to restore slavery in San Domingo, Toussaint resisted, but was compelled to surrender, and was sent to France, where he died in prison (1803).

P. 148.—"Tax not the royal Saint with vain expense." The royal Saint is Henry VI. This favourite (but to my mind much over-rated) sonnet is taken, together with "Walton's Book of Lives" and "Mutability," from the Ecclesiastical Sonnets, part iii. (1822).

P. 161.—"O lift with reverent hand that tarnished flower." "In a leaf of a quarto edition of the *Lives of the Saints*, written in Spanish by the learned and reverend father, Alfonso Villegas, Divine, of the Order of St. Dominick, set forth in English by John Heigham, Anno 1630, bought at a Catholic book-shop in Duke Street, Lincoln's Inn Fields, I found, carefully inserted, a painted flower, seemingly coeval with the book itself; and did not, for some time, discover that it opened in the middle, and was the cover to a very humble draught of a St. Anne, with the Virgin and Child; doubtless the performance of some poor but pious Catholic, whose meditations it assisted."—*Lamb's Note*.

P. 162.—"Mysterious Night! when our first parent knew." According to Coleridge "the finest and most grandly conceived sonnet in our language"; and according to Leigh Hunt, "Supreme, perhaps, above all in any language; nor can we ponder it too deeply, or with too hopeful a reverence."

NOTES

Blanco White's "Night and Death" is now the classical instance of a man's attaining to enduring poetic fame by a single sonnet. It is not that the rest of his writings fell far below, but that practically he exhausted himself with this one great stroke, and wrote no more. The largest information on "Night and Death" (which has quite a literature of its own) will be found in Mr. David M. Main's *Treasury of English Sonnets*.

P. 164.—"Green little vaulter in the sunny grass." Written in friendly rivalry with Keats, whose sonnet on the same subject will be found on p. 174.

P. 165.—"It flows through old hushed Ægypt and its sands." This, too, was written in friendly competition—with Keats and Shelley. To my mind, Hunt fairly worsted Keats in the *Grasshopper and Cricket* sonnet; but there can be no doubt at all that with his sonnet on the Nile he bore the palm away from the two greater poets. Here are the rival sonnets:

" Month after month the gathering rains descend,
　Drenching yon secret Ethiopian dells,
　And from the desert's ice-girt pinnacles
Where frost and heat in strange embraces blend
On Atlas, fields of moist snow half depend.
　Girt these with blasts and meteors, Tempest dwells
　By Nile's aerial urn ; with rapid spells
Urging those waters to their mighty end.
O'er Egypt's land of memory floods are level
　And they are thine, O Nile—and well thou knowest
That soul-sustaining airs and blasts of evil
　And fruits and poisons spring where'er thou flowest.
Beware, O Man—for knowledge must to thee
Like the great flood to Egypt ever be."—*Shelley*.

"Son of the old moon-mountains African !
　Chief of the Pyramid and Crocodile !
　We call thee fruitful, and, that very while,
A desert fills one seeing 's inward span ;
Nurse of swart nations since the world began,

212

NOTES

Art thou so fruitful?   Or dost thou beguile
Such men to honour thee, who, worn with toil,
Rest for a space 'twixt Cairo and Decan?
O may dark fancies err! they surely do;
'Tis ignorance that makes a barren waste
Of all beyond itself; thou dost bedew
Green rushes like our rivers, and dost taste
The pleasant sun-rise ; green isles hast thou too,
And to the sea as happily dost haste."—*Keats*.

P. 173.—"Much have I travelled in the realms
of gold."   Cowden Clarke records that in his
lodgings at Clerkenwell, one night in the summer
of 1815, he and Keats sat together till daylight
over a borrowed folio copy of Chapman's Homer ;
and that, when he came down to breakfast, at ten
o'clock next morning, he received this now famous
sonnet which Keats had found time to compose
and send from the Borough.

Line 11.—"Cortez" is of course a mistake.
The discoverer of the Pacific was Vasco Nunez
de Balboa, and the date of the discovery, 1513.

P. 174.—"The poetry of earth is never dead"—see
note on Leigh Hunt's sonnet, *supra*.

INDEX OF FIRST LINES

INDEX OF FIRST LINES

INDEX OF FIRST LINES

217

INDEX OF FIRST LINES

218

INDEX OF FIRST LINES

INDEX OF FIRST LINES

INDEX OF FIRST LINES

INDEX OF FIRST LINES

222

INDEX OF FIRST LINES